EVERYDAY EATING
WITH MURIEL AND ANDREW
"Our Favorite Meals Made Healthy and Delicious"

MURIEL ANGOT
WITH ANDREW LESSMAN

PHOTOGRAPHY: LINDSEY ELTINGE
FRONT COVER PHOTOGRAPHY: BRYAN KASM
BACK COVER PHOTOGRAPHY: ERIC COTSEN
STYLIST: LOETTA EARNEST
SOUS CHEF: JESUSITA MONTES
ASSISTANT: KYLE KLEIN
ART DIRECTION: EDWARD MOSS

Published by the Andrew Lessman Foundation
430 Parkson Road, Henderson, NV 89011

Printed in the United States of America.

First Printing, October 2014

ISBN 978-0-692-31467-8

Dedicated to enjoying the natural foods that insure our good health, since to do so, is the greatest gift we give ourselves and those we love.

ABOUT THE AUTHOR

 **Muriel Angot** was born and raised in the world's center of fine cuisine – Paris, France; however, it would take Muriel a couple of decades to rediscover her Parisian culinary roots, since she initially followed in her parents' footsteps studying Fine Art at the Sorbonne University in Paris. After college, Muriel's innate curiosity and desire to explore the world saw her leave France, spending time in Australia, Fiji, New Zealand and South America, until she fell in love with the United States where she established a beauty and wellness business in Aspen, Colorado. It wasn't until Muriel chose to attend cooking school that her true passion captured her and since that time, has never let go.

Like many French families, all the members of Muriel's family take pride in their abilities in the kitchen. But it was Muriel's paternal grandmother, Simone, who was to have the greatest influence, since she was the chef and owner of a restaurant in Picardie, France – a small city in the countryside just outside Paris. Some of Muriel's fondest childhood memories are of helping her grandmother create all the classic French dishes that were served at her restaurant. The special moments she shared with her grandmother in the culturally rich environment of an authentic French kitchen were to shape the rest of Muriel's life.

When Muriel moved from Colorado to California, the move presented an opportunity for a career change and with great trepidation she decided to take the plunge. Despite hearing how challenging and difficult it would be, Muriel followed her dream and attended Le Cordon Bleu cooking school in Paris – the same school attended by Julia Child. Ultimately, she graduated #1 in her class and now considers herself blessed to combine her two greatest passions – cooking and wellness.

FOREWORD
from Andrew and Muriel

Almost as frequently as I hear questions about vitamins, I am asked about my diet. As many of you know, as dedicated as I am to quality nutritional supplements, I am even more passionate about the food we eat. When I was a young athlete, I ate everything in sight with complete disregard for the health or quality of what I ate. My only concerns were the food's ability to fuel my athletic endeavors (the more calories the merrier) and support muscle tissue (tons of protein). Basically, I sought calories with a complete disregard for their quality and source. Fortunately, with age comes wisdom and now I always consider the consequences of the foods I eat, thus avoiding what I have always called dangerous "provocative" foods. For me, the most provocative foods are those that are highly processed and those with ingredients with a high glycemic index and added sugars or salt. Muriel and I share these same goals, since the science is now quite clear on how to eat for optimum energy and ideal weight.

Because Muriel and I eat so healthy, folks assume that our food must taste like cardboard. Nothing could be further from the truth. When friends and family eat at our home, they are always astounded that everything is so healthy, because it also tastes so delicious. Our prior books and their reviews are ample evidence that delicious food can still help you lose weight and ensure your best health. In this book, Muriel has revisited many of America's favorite foods and transformed them into healthy delicious meals. Whether it's pizza, sloppy Joes, mac and cheese, peanut butter and jelly, spaghetti and meatballs, apple pie or cheesecake. All these foods and a few dozen others are made healthy and delicious, and are easy to prepare. We have also removed most of the provocative ingredients I alluded to above. Specifically, even when called for, we add very little salt or sweetener to any recipe. We also do not use wheat or gluten nor typical pasta, rice, bread or even white potatoes or white rice.

Muriel and I have both always found that the more "unhealthy" foods or ingredients we eat, the more we want. Two perfect examples are salt and sugars. The less salt you use, the less salt you want. The more salt you use, the more salt you need to satisfy the conditioned taste for salt you have acquired. Today, I add little or no salt to foods and I consume a small fraction of the salt I did previously, but my food does not taste any less salty. Of course, we all need to consume a small amount of salt, but given the abundance of salt already in the foods we eat, there is little need to ever add salt to our diet. When it is called for, you can choose to add a small amount of salt to the recipes in this book, but Muriel and I add little or none and instead prefer the use of flavorful herbs.

Far worse than salt, is the presence of added sugars in the American diet. These sweet-tasting molecules are perhaps the most pernicious "addictive" ingredients in our diet. Although their manufacturers deny it, added sugars are at the very center of the epidemic of obesity in our society. For decades, I have said that today's soft drink and sugar industries are the equivalent of the tobacco industry in the 1960s. Like the tobacco industry back then, the soft drink industry and the folks behind the addition of sugars to all that we eat deny the harm their products cause. If these lies were not so deadly, they would be comic. In a few decades I expect, we will view these industries just as we did the tobacco industry. All human beings are born with a sweet tooth and these industries make us the victim of that genetically-coded potential "addiction." As Muriel and I have learned, the less we indulge our sweet tooth, the less we require. As a result, Muriel has created recipes (even desserts) that satisfy our sweet tooth while limiting the intake of sugars and high glycemic carbohydrates. Eliminating sugars and high glycemic carbs from our diet is perhaps the simplest way to lose weight – seemingly without trying.

Agribusiness, along with the packaged, processed and fast food industries have us all conditioned to want more and more high glycemic carbs and sugars. It was not that long ago that a foolish fear of fat triggered an even more foolish frenzy for low fat everything. The result was even more obesity due to foods richer in high glycemic carbs and sugars. When you combine this with larger portions, you have a recipe that guarantees an epidemic of obesity. Sadly, the most powerful producers of food in our society do not consider our health when they make products that ensure obesity and disease. It does not have to be that way. If we can reclaim control of what we put in our body, then weight loss and good health are the rewards we reap. The first step to reclaiming your health and ideal weight is to rescue your taste buds from the years of conditioning from agribusiness, processed food manufacturers and fast food companies. We are the victims of these enterprises. They have hijacked and seduced our taste buds and in so doing, robbed us of our good health. There is only one way to reclaim control of our own bodies and that is by refusing the foods and ingredients they offer. In so doing, you will learn that healthy actually means delicious. Once we discover the variety of flavors found in nature, particularly vegetables, herbs and spices and how to creatively combine them, we rediscover the wonderful human palate of our ancestors. We take back control of our health and the quality of our life from those who want to sell us their wares with absolutely no regard or regret about the fact that it is killing us.

I am sorry to be so direct about this issue, but unless Americans regain control of what we put in our bodies, then there is no greater threat to the quality of our life and the stability of our society than the health consequences of this epidemic of obesity. Even if you struggle with the quantity of food you put in your body, then the first step is as simple as changing the quality and nature of what you put in your body. As I always say, our best health does not begin with supplements, but with the food we choose every day to put in our body. I hope the everyday recipes in this book make it easier for you and those you love to reclaim your health from those who prefer to see you live otherwise.

Bon appétit!

Andrew and Muriel

Here are some of our favorite pictures of Lincoln.

CONTENTS

Smoothies

Breakfast

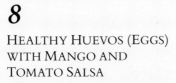

Breakfast *(continued)*

10
"GOOD MORNING" GLUTEN-FREE MUFFINS

11
HOMEMADE ALMOND BUTTER AND STRAWBERRY JAM (AB&J)

Appetizers

12
TURMERIC HUMMUS

13
SHRIMP SPRING ROLLS WITH SWEET CHILI SAUCE

14
TUNA SALAD ON A BED OF AVOCADO

15
ASIAN TURKEY MEATBALLS WITH SATAY SAUCE

16
ANGELICA'S FAVORITE DATE

Soups and Salads

17
"SOME LIKE IT HOT" CORN CHOWDER

18
EASY-TO-DO HOMEMADE CHICKEN VEGETABLE SOUP

Soups and Salads *(continued)*

19
SPINACH SALAD WITH STRAWBERRIES AND GOAT CHEESE

20
DELICIOUS CHINESE CHICKEN SALAD

21
GREEK SALAD WITH KALE AND WATERMELON

22
KOBB SALAD WITH SHRIMP

23
BROCCOLI SALAD WITH YELLOW RAISINS AND PINE NUTS

24
CHOPPED KALE CAESAR (KAESAR) SALAD WITH PARMESAN CRISPS

Main Dishes

25
MAPLE CHILI SALMON

26
TUNA BURGERS ON MUSHROOMS

27
FAUX-FRIED CHICKEN WITH WALNUTS AND THYME

28
OUR SWEET AND SOUR CHICKEN

29
EASY COQ AU VIN (CHICKEN IN WINE SAUCE)

30
ANDREW'S MEXICAN-STYLE CHICKEN BOWL

Main Dishes (continued)

31
Sloppy Joes on Cauliflower

32
Spaghetti Squash with Bison Meatballs

33
Tomato Marinara Sauce

34
Hearty Turkey Chili

35
Garbanzo and Cauliflower Crust Pizza

Side Dishes

36
Parsnips Mashed with Carrots

37
Green Beans with Walnuts and Queso Fresco

38
Quinoa Mac and Cheese with Cauliflower Béchamel

39
Zucchini Parmesan Fries

40
Carrot, Raisin and Oat Bread

41
Simple and Easy Cornbread

Desserts

ANDREW'S MULTI-BERRY "MILKSHAKE"

4 CUPS • PREPARATION: 5 MINUTES • VERY EASY

This is the first smoothie Andrew ever made for me. You can use his Vanilla Secure® Meal Replacement or his Whey Protein Isolate or any meal replacement or protein powder. He loves to add dark cherries when they are available, since they are, like all the other berries, so rich in protective compounds. He calls it his delicious berry milkshake and he often has it for breakfast or a snack or a quick source of post-workout protein. You can size it down to meet your needs. When Andrew makes this at home, all the fruits are generally frozen, so he just adds warm purified water to soften them up before blending. I often add flaxseed, chia seed or hemp protein when I make it myself.

1 scoop or packet Vanilla Secure®
    or 2 scoops Ultimate Whey
    Protein Isolate™ or protein
    powder of your choosing.

1 banana (preferably frozen)

1 cup blueberries

1 cup raspberries

1 cup blackberries

1 cup strawberries

1 cup water

1 cup ice

1 Place all ingredients in blender. Blend at high-speed until smooth, approximately 3 minutes.

2 Serve immediately.

Nutrition Information

Serving Size **1 Cup**　　　　　　　　　　　Servings **4**

Calories **103**	Potassium . . . . . . **214 mg**
Calories from fat **7**	Total Carbohydrates . . . **17 g**
Total Fat . . . . **1 g**	Dietary Fiber . . . . **3 g**
Cholesterol . . . . **0 mg**	Sugars . . . . **10 g**
Sodium . . . . **36 mg**	Protein . . . . **8 g**

Vitamin A . . . . **3 %**	Folic Acid. . . . . **22 %**
Vitamin C . . . . **71 %**	Vitamin B12. . . . . . **50 %**
Calcium . . . . **9 %**	Biotin. . . . . **13 %**
Iron . . . . **3 %**	Pantothenic Acid . . . **14 %**
Vitamin D . . . . **13 %**	Phosphorus. . . . . **5 %**
Vitamin E. . . . . . . **41 %**	Magnesium. . . . . . . **11 %**
Vitamin K . . . . **9 %**	Zinc . . . . **4 %**
Vitamin B1. . . . . . . **31 %**	Selenium . . . . **9 %**
Vitamin B2. . . . . . . **20 %**	Copper . . . . **4 %**
Niacin . . . . **27 %**	Manganese . . . . **18 %**
Vitamin B6. . . . . . . **30 %**	

OTHER BENEFICIAL NUTRIENTS (PER SERVING)

Omega-3 (ALA+EPA+DPA+DHA). . **21 mg**	
Choline. . . . . **7 mg**	
Beta-Carotene . . . . **22 mcg**	
Alpha-Carotene . . . . **7 mcg**	
Lutein & Zeaxanthin . . . . **45 mcg**	

ANGI'S NUTRITIOUS SPINACH AND KALE MATCHA GREEN SMOOTHIE

4 CUPS • PREPARATION: 5 MINUTES • VERY EASY

My wonderful girlfriend, Angi from Aspen, makes this delicious kale and spinach Matcha Green Tea Smoothie every morning. The almond butter and flaxseed are nutritious and filling, and the Spinach and Kale are among the best sources of Lutein and Zeaxanthin. The Matcha Green Tea provides the exceptional protection of EGCG. You can use Andrew's Vanilla Secure® Complete Meal Replacement or his Whey Protein Isolate or any meal replacement or protein powder of your choosing. The almond milk and honey are optional, but add some nice creaminess or sweetness if required. This Green Smoothie is one of our favorite ways to start the day!

1 scoop or packet Vanilla Secure®
  or 2 scoops Ultimate Whey
  Protein Isolate™ or protein
  powder of your choosing.
1 frozen banana

1 tsp. honey (optional)
1 tbsp. almond butter
2 kale leaves (remove the bitter
  stem)
2 cups fresh spinach

1 tbsp. flaxseeds
1½ cups almond milk
1 tbsp. Matcha Green
  Tea Powder
1 cup ice

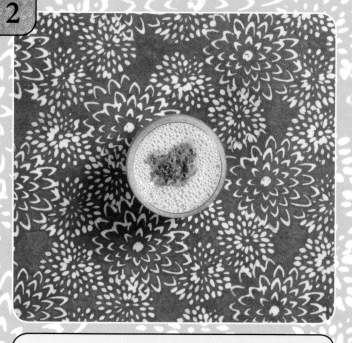

1 Place all ingredients in blender. Blend at high-speed until smooth, approximately 3 minutes.

2 Serve immediately.

Nutrition Information

Serving Size **1 Cup**　　　　　　　　　　Servings **4**

Calories **151**	Potassium . . . . . **438 mg**
Calories from fat **33**	Total Carbohydrates . . . **18 g**
Total Fat . . . . **4 g**	Dietary Fiber . . . . **3 g**
Cholesterol . . . . **2 mg**	Sugars . . . . **12 g**
Sodium . . . . **88 mg**	Protein . . . . **12 g**

Vitamin A . . . . **43 %**	Folic Acid. . . . . . . **29 %**
Vitamin C . . . . **45 %**	Vitamin B12 . . . . . . **58 %**
Calcium . . . . **24 %**	Biotin. . . . . **13 %**
Iron . . . . **6 %**	Pantothenic Acid. . . **17 %**
Vitamin D . . . . **16 %**	Phosphorus. . . . . . . **17 %**
Vitamin E. . . . . **46 %**	Magnesium. . . . . . . **27 %**
Vitamin K . . . . . . **126 %**	Zinc . . . . **7 %**
Vitamin B1. . . . . . . **36 %**	Selenium . . . . **14 %**
Vitamin B2. . . . . . . **33 %**	Copper. . . . . **10 %**
Niacin . . . . **28 %**	Manganese . . . . . . **20 %**
Vitamin B6. . . . . . . **33 %**	

OTHER BENEFICIAL NUTRIENTS (PER SERVING)

Choline. . . . . **24 mg**
Beta-Carotene. . . . . **1,090 mcg**
Alpha-Carotene . . . . **11 mcg**
Lutein & Zeaxanthin. . . . . **2,177 mcg**

TROPICAL PAPAYA AND PINEAPPLE SMOOTHIE

4 CUPS • PREPARATION: 5 MINUTES • VERY EASY

Andrew loves to talk about the abundant and diverse nutrition one gets from a colorful diet. There are no better examples than the first three smoothies in this book. First, the rich red colors of berries and then the deep green of spinach and kale followed by the orange and yellow of papaya and pineapple. We often alternate these three smoothies to have a healthy and "colorful" week. I use the Piña Colada Secure® Meal Replacement for extra flavor, but it is also delicious with Vanilla Secure® or Andrew's Whey Protein Isolate. Papaya is rich in enzymes and protective compounds. We also sometimes add fresh mango or some segments from an orange or grapefruit for some additional orange-colored nutrition.

1 scoop or packet Piña Colada
    Secure® or 2 scoops Ultimate
    Whey Protein Isolate™
    or protein powder of
    your choosing.

2 fresh papayas

1 cup frozen pineapple

½ banana (preferably frozen)

1 cup ice

1 cup coconut water
    or plain water

1 Place all ingredients in blender. Blend at high-speed until smooth, approximately 3 minutes.

2 Serve immediately.

Nutrition Information

Serving Size **1 Cup**   Servings **4**

Calories **115**	Potassium . . . . . . **274 mg**
Calories from fat **7**	Total Carbohydrates . . . **20 g**
Total Fat . . . . **1 g**	Dietary Fiber . . . . **3 g**
Cholesterol . . . . **0 mg**	Sugars . . . . **14 g**
Sodium . . . . **42 mg**	Protein . . . . **8 g**

Vitamin A . . . . **18 %**	Folic Acid. . . . . **28 %**
Vitamin C . . . . . . **140 %**	Vitamin B12. . . . . . **50 %**
Calcium . . . . **10 %**	Biotin. . . . . **13 %**
Iron . . . . **3 %**	Pantothenic Acid . . . **15 %**
Vitamin D . . . . **13 %**	Phosphorus. . . . . **5 %**
Vitamin E. . . . . . . **40 %**	Magnesium. . . . . . . **14 %**
Vitamin K . . . . . . **4 %**	Zinc . . . . **3 %**
Vitamin B1. . . . . . **33 %**	Selenium . . . . **10 %**
Vitamin B2. . . . . . **20 %**	Copper . . . . **6 %**
Niacin . . . . **28 %**	Manganese . . . . **24 %**
Vitamin B6. . . . . . . **30 %**	

OTHER BENEFICIAL NUTRIENTS (PER SERVING)

Choline.	**9 mg**
Beta-Carotene	**234 mcg**
Alpha-Carotene	**6 mcg**
Lutein & Zeaxanthin	**74 mcg**
Lycopene.	**1,435 mcg**

CHOCOLATE CINNAMON SMOOTHIE

4 CUPS • PREPARATION: 5 MINUTES • VERY EASY

I love the taste of Chocolate, which makes me a huge fan of Andrew's Chocolate Secure® Meal Replacement. Of course, you can feel free to use your own chocolate meal replacement or a protein powder of your choosing. I love the combination of cinnamon with chocolate and Andrew always reminds me how healthy cinnamon can be for so many systems in our body, particularly for healthy insulin balance and blood sugar metabolism. Chocolate is also rich in protective compounds and chocolate nibs are their most concentrated source. For me, this smoothie is like having a healthy chocolate milkshake.

1 scoop or packet Chocolate Secure®
   or 2 scoops Ultimate Whey
   Protein Isolate™ or protein
   powder of your choosing.

1 tbsp. cashew butter
1 tsp. cinnamon
1 banana (preferably frozen)
1 tbsp. flaxseed

1½ cups coconut water
1 tbsp. cacao nibs
1 cup ice
1 tsp. vanilla

1 Place all ingredients in blender. Blend at high-speed until smooth, approximately 3 minutes.

2 Serve immediately.

Nutrition Information

Serving Size **1 Cup**   Servings **4**

Calories	**123**	Potassium	**421 mg**
Calories from fat	**44**	Total Carbohydrates	**16 g**
Total Fat	**5 g**	Dietary Fiber	**4 g**
Cholesterol	**0 mg**	Sugars	**8 g**
Sodium	**112 mg**	Protein	**4 g**

Vitamin A	**3 %**	Folic Acid	**16 %**
Vitamin C	**33 %**	Vitamin B12	**50 %**
Calcium	**10 %**	Biotin	**13 %**
Iron	**8 %**	Pantothenic Acid	**15 %**
Vitamin D	**13 %**	Phosphorus	**8 %**
Vitamin E	**39 %**	Magnesium	**20 %**
Vitamin K	**1 %**	Zinc	**6 %**
Vitamin B1	**18 %**	Selenium	**12 %**
Vitamin B2	**18 %**	Copper	**13 %**
Niacin	**15 %**	Manganese	**24 %**
Vitamin B6	**20 %**		

OTHER BENEFICIAL NUTRIENTS (PER SERVING)

Omega-3 (ALA+EPA+DPA+DHA)	**1 mg**
Choline	**5 mg**
Beta-Carotene	**9 mcg**
Alpha-Carotene	**8 mcg**
Lutein & Zeaxanthin	**20 mcg**

MURIEL'S "GET YOU GOING" DATE AND COFFEE SMOOTHIE

4 CUPS • PREPARATION: 5 MINUTES • VERY EASY

Andrew and I mostly speak French, but for this smoothie he taught me the following American expression: "When the going gets tough, the tough get going." So, this is my smoothie for when the going gets tough and you prefer to get going. I love the flavor of Andrew's Coffee Secure® Meal Replacement and because it contains real coffee, it has a bit of real caffeine, which can definitely get you going. The rich fiber contained in the chia seeds, flaxseeds and date, or the figs we sometimes choose to add, can also help move things along. You can of course use your own protein powder and for the coffee flavor, a teaspoon or two of instant coffee can work in lieu of the Secure. For me, this smoothie tastes like a coffee ice cream shake.

1 scoop or packet Coffee Secure®
or 2 scoops Ultimate Whey
Protein Isolate™ or protein
powder of your choosing.

½ banana (preferably frozen)

1 pitted date

1 tbsp. almond butter

1 cup ice

1½ cups water
(or almond milk or
skim milk)

1 tbsp. chia and flaxseeds

1 Place all ingredients in blender. Blend at high-speed until smooth, approximately 3 minutes.

2 Serve immediately.

Nutrition Information

Serving Size **1 Cup** Servings **4**

Calories	96	Potassium	147 mg
Calories from fat	31	Total Carbohydrates	8 g
Total Fat	3 g	Dietary Fiber	2 g
Cholesterol	0 mg	Sugars	5 g
Sodium	36 mg	Protein	8 g

Vitamin A	3 %	Folic Acid	20 %
Vitamin C	27 %	Vitamin B12	50 %
Calcium	10 %	Biotin	13 %
Iron	3 %	Pantothenic Acid	13 %
Vitamin D	13 %	Phosphorus	7 %
Vitamin E	44 %	Magnesium	13 %
Vitamin K	1 %	Zinc	4 %
Vitamin B1	32 %	Selenium	10 %
Vitamin B2	21 %	Copper	5 %
Niacin	26 %	Manganese	10 %
Vitamin B6	28 %		

OTHER BENEFICIAL NUTRIENTS (PER SERVING)

Choline	5 mg
Beta-Carotene	5 mcg
Alpha-Carotene	4 mcg
Lutein & Zeaxanthin	17 mcg

HEALTHY HI-FIBER PANCAKE

2 SERVINGS • PREPARATION: 8 MINUTES • COOKING: 10 MINUTES • EASY

I have been making these healthy pancakes for more than a decade. It's everyone's favorite breakfast when we have visitors at the house. It is incredibly easy to make and its assortment of ingredients makes it a great source of comprehensive nutrition and a wonderfully healthy way to start the day. Like the prior smoothie, its rich fiber content tends to help keep things moving right along. I used to always make it with a crushed banana, but now prefer to use cottage cheese. You can see what works best for you and of course, I encourage you to experiment adding fruit, berries or other ingredients of your choosing.

1 tsp. coconut oil	½ tsp. cinnamon	A few pecans, chopped
⅓ cup oat bran	½ tsp. vanilla extract	½ cup fresh fruit
⅓ cup cottage cheese (or ½ mashed banana)	1 tbsp. flaxseeds	Maple syrup, as desired
3 egg whites	¼ cup blueberries (fresh or frozen)	

1 In a bowl, whisk together the oat bran, cottage cheese, egg whites, cinnamon, vanilla and flaxseeds.

2 Melt coconut oil in a small, non-stick skillet over medium heat and pour half of the batter into the pan. Add half of the blueberries and pecans to each serving and cook for 5 minutes.

3 Carefully, flip the pancake with a spatula and cook for an additional 5 minutes at medium-low heat.

4 Serve with fresh fruits and maple syrup. Delicious!

Nutrition Information

Serving Size **1 Pancake**   Servings **2**

Calories	**262**	Potassium	**26 mg**
Calories from fat	**21**	Total Carbohydrates	**6 g**
Total Fat	**8 g**	Dietary Fiber	**9 g**
Cholesterol	**199 mg**	Sugars	**14 g**
Sodium	**430 mg**	Protein	**14 g**
Vitamin C	**44 %**	Vitamin B6	**1389 %**
Iron	**5 %**	Iodine	**155 %**
Vitamin E	**25 %**	Phosphorus	**8 %**
Vitamin B1	**29 %**	Zinc	**141 %**
Vitamin B2	**48 %**	Copper	**89 %**
Niacin	**1 %**		

OTHER BENEFICIAL NUTRIENTS (PER SERVING)

Omega-3 (ALA+EPA+DPA+DHA) **1,068mg**

Choline . . . . **24 mg**

Beta-Carotene . . . . **9 mcg**

Alpha-Carotene . . . . **75 mcg**

ANDREW'S OMELETTE WITH MUSHROOMS, TOMATOES, SWISS CHEESE AND HERBS

1 SERVING • PREPARATION: 8 MINUTES • COOKING: 8 MINUTES • EASY

One of the first things I ever prepared for Andrew was a proper Omelette à la Française. In France, we take our omelettes very seriously and I can still remember my grandma showing me how to correctly make an omelette as a child. Andrew loved how much care I took in utilizing a wide assortment of fine herbs and of course, you can experiment and expand on the herbs listed below to suit your taste. Andrew and I have found that we can avoid using salt by using a nice mélange of herbs. Andrew's favorite Swiss cheese is called Jarlsberg, but you can replace it with your own favorite cheese, just avoid overly processed cheeses. Personally, I only use egg whites, but for Andrew, I will often use just one egg yolk.

1 tsp. olive oil

½ cup mushrooms, chopped

½ cup cherry tomatoes, halved

1 egg + 2 egg whites

¼ cup Jarlsberg or Swiss cheese, shredded

1 oz. fresh chives

1 oz. fresh thyme

Salt and freshly ground black pepper to taste

1 Add half the olive oil to a nonstick pan over medium heat and sauté the mushrooms and tomatoes for approximately 4 minutes. Remove the vegetables to a side plate and reserve. Wipe the skillet clean and add remaining olive oil.

2 Whisk egg and whites in a small bowl for 30 seconds until slightly frothy.

3 Pour eggs into the skillet over medium heat and, working quickly with a rubber spatula, gently pull the coagulated egg from the sides of the pan towards the runny, uncooked center. Repeat until the eggs cook to the desired consistency.

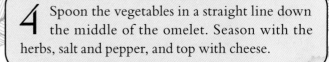

4 Spoon the vegetables in a straight line down the middle of the omelet. Season with the herbs, salt and pepper, and top with cheese.

5 With your spatula, carefully lift one edge of the omelette and fold it across and over, so that the edges line up. Gently slide the omelette from the pan onto a plate and serve with a slice of our delicious Carrot, Raisin and Oat Bread (Recipe 40). Voila!

Nutrition Information

Serving Size **1 Omelette**   Servings **1**

Calories	**299**	Potassium	**749 mg**
Calories from fat	**157**	Total Carbohydrates	**12 g**
Total Fat	**17 g**	Dietary Fiber	**3 g**
Cholesterol	**211 mg**	Sugars	**7 g**
Sodium	**245 mg**	Protein	**23 g**

Vitamin A	**44 %**	Vitamin B6	**14 %**
Vitamin C	**48 %**	Folic Acid	**16 %**
Calcium	**27 %**	Vitamin B12	**23 %**
Iron	**11 %**	Pantothenic Acid	**17 %**
Vitamin D	**13 %**	Phosphorus	**35 %**
Vitamin E	**11 %**	Magnesium	**14 %**
Vitamin K	**30 %**	Zinc	**17 %**
Vitamin B1	**8 %**	Selenium	**50 %**
Vitamin B2	**42 %**	Copper	**11 %**
Niacin	**13 %**	Manganese	**17 %**

OTHER BENEFICIAL NUTRIENTS (PER SERVING)

Omega-3 (ALA+EPA+DPA+DHA)	**85 mg**
Choline	**164 mg**
Beta-Carotene	**951 mcg**
Alpha-Carotene	**182 mcg**
Lutein & Zeaxanthin	**483 mcg**
Lycopene	**4,631 mcg**

HEALTHY HUEVOS (EGGS) WITH MANGO AND TOMATO SALSA

4 SERVINGS • PREPARATION: 15 MINUTES • COOKING: 20 MINUTES • MEDIUM

"Huevos Rancheros" have always been one of my favorite breakfasts, but when I saw the high calorie content, I almost passed out. I decided then and there that I had to make a lighter, healthier version of this breakfast favorite. Mangos are a delicious and antioxidant-rich fruit that make a delicious salsa, which I sometimes replace with a kiwi, papaya or pineapple to make an equally tasty salsa. These fruit salsas also make a wonderful condiment alongside fish or chicken. Cook your eggs any way you want, but we usually prefer poached or over easy.

Salsa:

1 mango, peeled and chopped

1 jalapeño, sliced (reserve a few
    slices for garnish)

Juice of 1 lime

1 cup cherry tomatoes, halved

1 oz. fresh cilantro, chopped

¼ cup scallions, chopped

Beans:

15 oz. can black beans, rinsed

1 shallot

1 garlic clove

2 tsp. olive oil

Salt and freshly ground black
    pepper to taste

4 eggs

¾ cup queso fresco

4 small corn tortillas

1 Mix all the salsa ingredients together. Cover and chill.

2 Add a little olive oil to a skillet over medium heat and sauté the shallots and garlic for 5 minutes. Add the cooked beans, salt and pepper, and a few slices of jalapeño, if desired, sautéing for an additional 5 minutes until hot and well mixed.

3 Add a little olive oil to a sauté pan over medium heat, break an egg into the pan, season with salt and pepper, and cook for 5 minutes.

4 Warm the tortillas in a pan with a little olive oil, heating for 5 minutes each.

5 Place a tortilla on a plate, add a 1/2 cup of beans. Add the egg, cover with salsa, and top with queso fresco. Garnish with a slice of jalapeño and a few leaves of cilantro. Voila!

Nutrition Information

Servings **4**

Calories	**407**	Potassium	**763 mg**
Calories from fat	**134**	Total Carbohydrates	**48 g**
Total Fat	**15 g**	Dietary Fiber	**10 g**
Cholesterol	**202 mg**	Sugars	**15 g**
Sodium	**561 mg**	Protein	**21 g**

Vitamin A	**38 %**	Vitamin B6	**15 %**
Vitamin C	**77 %**	Folic Acid	**42 %**
Calcium	**24 %**	Vitamin B12	**14 %**
Iron	**23 %**	Pantothenic Acid	**13 %**
Vitamin D	**17 %**	Phosphorus	**38 %**
Vitamin E	**14 %**	Magnesium	**18 %**
Vitamin K	**4 %**	Zinc	**14 %**
Vitamin B1	**23 %**	Selenium	**40 %**
Vitamin B2	**28 %**	Copper	**20 %**
Niacin	**13 %**	Manganese	**26 %**

OTHER BENEFICIAL NUTRIENTS (PER SERVING)

Choline	**187 mg**
Beta-Carotene	**849 mcg**
Alpha-Carotene	**56 mcg**
Lutein & Zeaxanthin	**440 mcg**
Lycopene	**1,160 mcg**

BREAKFAST BOWL WITH QUINOA, SPINACH AND EGGS

4 SERVINGS • PREPARATION: 5 MINUTES • COOKING: 30 MINUTES • MEDIUM

This is my healthier and tastier version of one of Andrew's favorite breakfast bowls at a local restaurant. It contains nutrient-rich quinoa (one of our favorite ingredients), along with spinach (a favorite of Andrew's) and other vegetables and spices. Andrew just loves the combination of ingredients. A single egg per serving is a light meal and offers a good source of protein, while two eggs per serving will make for a great protein-rich, post-workout meal.

1 cup water

½ cup dry quinoa

1 tsp. olive oil

1 zucchini, sliced

1 cup yellow cherry tomatoes
(halved)

Salt and freshly ground black
pepper to taste

½ tsp. Five Spice powder

1 capful white vinegar

2 to 4 eggs
(1 or 2 eggs per serving)

2 cups spinach

½ tsp. paprika

¼ tsp. chili flakes (optional)

1 Cook the quinoa according to the package. Typically, it is one cup of water to ½ cup of quinoa, which you bring to a boil, then reduce heat, cover and simmer for 15 minutes.

2 Add 1 tsp. olive oil to a small skillet over medium heat and sauté the zucchini and tomatoes with salt and pepper for approximately 5 minutes. Mix with the quinoa, Five Spice powder, and additional salt and pepper to taste, if desired.

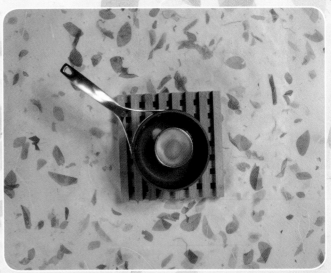

3 In a small saucepan over medium heat, bring 2 to 3 inches of water to a gentle boil. Add a capful of white vinegar. Place an egg ring in the center of the pan.

4 Crack an egg into a ramequin or small dish, and gently slide into the egg ring. Reduce heat and cover, poaching the egg for approximately 4 minutes for soft to medium firmness.

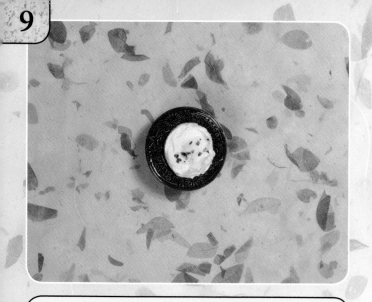

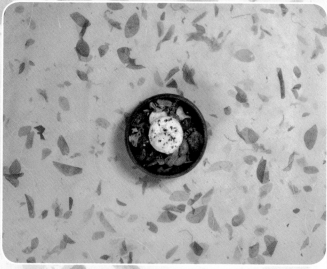

5 Carefully scoop the egg out of the water with a slotted spoon, placing on a strong paper towel to drain. Gently pat the top of the egg with another paper towel to remove any excess water.

6 Toss the spinach with the quinoa and vegetables, and separate into bowls, topping each with a poached egg, sprinkling with paprika and chili flakes.

Nutrition Information

Serving Size **1 Bowl**   Servings **4**

Calories 199	Potassium . . . . . . 495 mg
Calories from fat 84	Total Carbohydrates . . . 18 g
Total Fat . . . . 9 g	Dietary Fiber . . . . 7 g
Cholesterol . . . . . 186 mg	Sugars . . . . 3 g
Sodium . . . . 116 mg	Protein . . . . 11 g

Vitamin A . . . . 45 %	Folic Acid. . . . . 27 %
Vitamin C . . . . 30 %	Vitamin B12. . . . . . . 7 %
Calcium . . . . 7 %	Pantothenic Acid . . . 11 %
Iron . . . . 15 %	Phosphorus. . . . . . . 23 %
Vitamin D . . . . 10 %	Magnesium. . . . . . . 18 %
Vitamin E. . . . . 9 %	Zinc . . . . 11 %
Vitamin B1. . . . . . . 10 %	Selenium . . . . 25 %
Vitamin B2. . . . . . . 22 %	Copper. . . . . 12 %
Niacin . . . . 5 %	Manganese . . . . 36 %
Vitamin B6. . . . . . . 12 %	

OTHER BENEFICIAL NUTRIENTS (PER SERVING)

Omega-3 (ALA+EPA+DPA+DHA). . **89 mg**	
Choline. . . . . **172 mg**	
Beta-Carotene . . . . **1,147 mcg**	
Alpha-Carotene . . . . **39 mcg**	
Lutein & Zeaxanthin . . . . **3,257 mcg**	
Lycopene. . . . . **958 mcg**	

"Good Morning" Gluten-Free Muffins

12 MUFFINS • PREPARATION: 15 MINUTES • COOKING: 20 MINUTES • EASY

My Mom was visiting from Paris and as usual, we found ourselves in the kitchen, this time experimenting with different muffin recipes. This recipe with carrots, raisins and walnuts was her favorite and it was so good, I had to add it to this cookbook. Unlike so many muffins out in the supermarket with questionable ingredients, this muffin is both delicious and healthy. It also works equally well with zucchini and pecans, and Andrew prefers them when I add some coconut flakes.

Cooking oil spray

1¼ cups oat flour

½ cup oat bran

½ tsp. salt

¾ cup brown sugar

1 tsp. baking soda

1 tsp. baking powder

1 tsp. cinnamon

1 cup almond milk or low-fat buttermilk

2 eggs (or 4 egg whites)

¼ cup coconut oil, canola oil, or butter

1 cup carrots, grated

½ cup yellow raisins

¼ cup walnuts, chopped

1 tbsp. rolled oats

1 Preheat oven to 350°. Place paper liners in a 12-count muffin tin and lightly spray with cooking oil. In a large bowl, mix the flour, bran, salt, brown sugar, baking soda, baking powder and cinnamon.

2 In a smaller bowl, whisk together the milk, eggs and oil.

3 Fold the wet ingredients into the dry. DON'T OVERMIX! Fold in the carrots, raisins and walnuts.

4 Divide the batter among the muffin cups and sprinkle a few rolled oats on the tops. Bake approximately 20 minutes until the muffins are puffy and golden, and a toothpick comes out clean.

5 Serve with our homemade Jam (Recipe 11). They're delicious!

Nutrition Information

Serving Size **1 Muffin**   Servings **12**

Calories	**105**	Potassium	**141 mg**
Calories from fat	**51**	Total Carbohydrates	**9 g**
Total Fat	**6 g**	Dietary Fiber	**1 g**
Cholesterol	**76 mg**	Sugars	**3 g**
Sodium	**187 mg**	Protein	**4 g**

Vitamin A	**18 %**	Folic Acid	**4 %**
Vitamin C	**1 %**	Vitamin B12	**4 %**
Calcium	**3 %**	Pantothenic Acid	**4 %**
Iron	**4 %**	Phosphorus	**11 %**
Vitamin D	**5 %**	Magnesium	**6 %**
Vitamin E	**2 %**	Zinc	**4 %**
Vitamin B1	**6 %**	Selenium	**14 %**
Vitamin B2	**8 %**	Copper	**4 %**
Niacin	**1 %**	Manganese	**21 %**
Vitamin B6	**2 %**		

OTHER BENEFICIAL NUTRIENTS (PER SERVING)

Omega-3 (ALA+EPA+DPA+DHA)	**23 mg**
Choline	**65 mg**
Beta-Carotene	**380 mcg**
Alpha-Carotene	**159 mcg**
Lutein & Zeaxanthin	**128 mcg**

HOMEMADE ALMOND BUTTER AND STRAWBERRY JAM (AB&J)

ALMOND BUTTER: 1 1/2 CUPS • PREPARATION: 5 MINUTES • EASY
JAM: 4 CUPS • PREPARATION: 7 MINUTES • COOKING: 10–12 MINUTES • EASY

Andrew has never been a big fan of peanut butter, so I had to come up with a new healthy version of everyone's favorite PB&J sandwich. We call this one our AB&J sandwich. Its ingredients go perfectly with my pancakes, muffins or our carrot bread. We start with almond butter, which is surprisingly easy to make at home and is also my favorite snack food. In minutes, I can eat a good-sized bowl while working in the kitchen! It just disappears! You can also replace the almonds with cashews to make a delicious CB&J. As for the jam (jelly), I used berries here, because they go so well with almond butter, but you can choose to use your favorite fruit. I also add figs (or dates) because they add sweetness and their fiber content provides a nice texture. Once created, the almond butter should be stored in a sealed container in the refrigerator. I only make small batches that last a few weeks, so it stays fresh.

Almond Butter:

12 oz. roasted almonds

1 tsp. canola oil

Jam:

1 cup figs, chopped

3 cups strawberries or
mixed berries

1 tbsp. agave

Juice of 1 lemon and zest

1 tbsp. water

1 Mix the nuts and oil together in a food processor for approximately 5 minutes. Scrape the sides a few times during the process.

2 Add all the jam ingredients to a small saucepan.

3 Bring the jam to a gentle boil, reduce heat and simmer for approximately 10 minutes.

4 To make the jam extra smooth, you can also place it in a blender and pulse a few times.

5 Spread the jam and almond butter on a slice of our Carrot, Raisin and Oat Bread (Recipe 40) and voila!

Almond Butter Nutrition Information

Serving Size **1 Tablespoon** Servings **16**

Calories	**134**	Potassium	**150 mg**
Calories from fat	**97**	Total Carbohydrates	**5 g**
Total Fat	**11 g**	Dietary Fiber	**3 g**
Cholesterol	**0 mg**	Sugars	**1 g**
Sodium	**0 mg**	Protein	**5 g**

Calcium	**6 %**	Pantothenic Acid	**1 %**
Iron	**4 %**	Phosphorus	**10 %**
Vitamin E	**28 %**	Magnesium	**14 %**
Vitamin B1	**3 %**	Zinc	**4 %**
Vitamin B2	**13 %**	Selenium	**1 %**
Niacin	**4 %**	Copper	**11 %**
Vitamin B6	**2 %**	Manganese	**24 %**
Folic Acid	**3 %**		

OTHER BENEFICIAL NUTRIENTS (PER SERVING)

Omega-3 (ALA+EPA+DPA+DHA)	**27 mg**
Choline	**11 mg**

Jam Nutrition Information

Serving Size **1 Tablespoon** Servings **24**

Calories	**28**	Potassium	**72 mg**
Calories from fat	**2**	Total Carbohydrates	**6 g**
Total Fat	**0 g**	Dietary Fiber	**1 g**
Cholesterol	**0 mg**	Sugars	**4 g**
Sodium	**1 mg**	Protein	**0 g**

Vitamin C	**19 %**	Vitamin B6	**1 %**
Calcium	**1 %**	Folic Acid	**1 %**
Iron	**1 %**	Pantothenic Acid	**1 %**
Vitamin E	**1 %**	Phosphorus	**1 %**
Vitamin B1	**1 %**	Magnesium	**2 %**
Vitamin B2	**1 %**	Copper	**1 %**
Niacin	**1 %**	Manganese	**5 %**

OTHER BENEFICIAL NUTRIENTS (PER SERVING)

Choline	**2 mg**
Beta-Carotene	**3 mcg**
Lutein & Zeaxanthin	**5 mcg**

TURMERIC HUMMUS

2 CUPS • PREPARATION: 7 MINUTES • VERY EASY

One of Andrew's and my favorite snacks and dips is hummus. Since Andrew has always been a huge proponent of Turmeric and all its health benefits, I thought I'd try to create a delicious combination offering the texture of hummus and the flavor of Turmeric. It came out perfectly! In fact, we never eat plain hummus anymore and instead, enjoy our new Turmeric hummus. I have also created two other delicious versions with roasted red, orange and yellow peppers or the Japanese spice – wasabi. We use it as a veggie dip or Andrew will eat it alongside fish or chicken. Of course, you can use more or less cayenne depending on the desired "warmth."

15 oz. can garbanzo beans, rinsed	1 tsp. cumin	Juice of 1 lemon and a little zest
1 tbsp. tahini	1½ tsp. turmeric	Kosher salt and freshly ground pepper
1 clove garlic	¼ tsp. cayenne	
	2 tbsp. fat-free yogurt	¼ cup toasted pine nuts

1 In a blender or food processor, add all the ingredients, except the pine nuts, and mix for about 4 minutes until the mixture forms a smooth paste.

2 Serve in a bowl, garnished with toasted pine nuts and a little cayenne or turmeric. I serve with cut vegetables such as broccoli, cauliflower, endive, radish and carrots, or crackers.

Nutrition Information

Serving Size **1 Tablespoon**   Servings **32**

Calories **25**	Potassium . . . . **28 mg**
Calories from fat **12**	Total Carbohydrates . . . . **2 g**
Total Fat . . . . **1 g**	Dietary Fiber . . . . **1 g**
Cholesterol . . . . **0 mg**	Sugars . . . . **1 g**
Sodium . . . . **19 mg**	Protein . . . . **1 g**

Vitamin C . . . . **1 %**	Vitamin B6 . . . . **1 %**
Calcium . . . . **1 %**	Folic Acid . . . . **1 %**
Iron . . . . **2 %**	Phosphorus . . . . **2 %**
Vitamin E . . . . **1 %**	Magnesium . . . . **1 %**
Vitamin K . . . . **1 %**	Zinc . . . . **1 %**
Vitamin B1 . . . . **1 %**	Copper . . . . **2 %**
Vitamin B2 . . . . **1 %**	Manganese . . . . **9 %**

OTHER BENEFICIAL NUTRIENTS (PER SERVING)

Omega-3 (ALA+EPA+DPA+DHA) . . . **1 mg**

Choline . . . . **1 mg**

Beta-Carotene . . . . **5 mcg**

Lutein & Zeaxanthin . . . . **2 mcg**

SHRIMP SPRING ROLLS
WITH SWEET CHILI SAUCE

8 ROLLS • PREPARATION: 35-45 MINUTES • COOKING: 5 MINUTES • MEDIUM TO DIFFICULT

Because of the rice paper, this is a little bit more time consuming than my typical quick recipes, but everyone who has tried it has told me it is really worth the effort. This is a light, fresh and healthy appetizer! I try not to make too many of them, since everyone likes them so much, they will fill up on these before dinner. I really enjoy the sweet-and-spicy chili sauce, but Andrew also likes it when I replace it with our Satay Sauce (Recipe 15) for added creaminess.

Shrimp Spring Rolls:

2 oz. rice vermicelli

10 rice paper wraps
 (approximately 8" diameter)

1 oz. fresh mint leaves

1 oz. fresh cilantro leaves

1 head Bibb lettuce

10 medium shrimp, cooked and
 halved lengthwise

¼ cup roasted peanuts or cashews

1 lime

Sweet Chili Sauce:

2 tbsp. fish sauce

2 tbsp. rice wine vinegar

2 tbsp. lime juice

2 tbsp. agave

1 garlic clove, crushed

1 red hot chili

1 Fill a small saucepan with water and bring to a boil. Pour the water into a bowl and add the vermicelli. Soak for approximately 5 minutes, then drain and set aside.

2 Fill another bowl with hot water and, working one at a time, dip each rice wrap in it for 1 minute. Remove and lay the wraps flat on a moist paper towel.

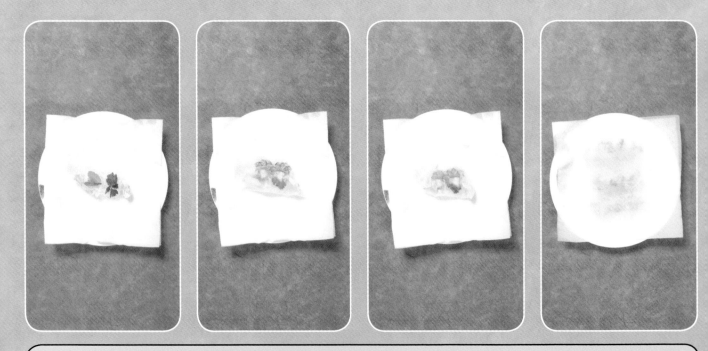

3 In the center of each wrap, add the vermicelli, mint, cilantro, lettuce, shrimp and a few nuts. Fold the sides of each wrap inward and then tightly roll. Keep under a moist paper towel until all the wraps are rolled.

4 For the sweet chili sauce, whisk all the ingredients together at once.

5 Serve with fresh sliced lime and peanuts with the sauce on the side.

Nutrition Information

Serving Size **1 Roll**   Servings **8**

Calories **78**	Potassium . . . . . . **145 mg**
Calories from fat **16**	Total Carbohydrates . . . **13 g**
Total Fat . . . . **2 g**	Dietary Fiber . . . . **1 g**
Cholesterol . . . . . . **10 mg**	Sugars . . . . **5 g**
Sodium . . . . **483 mg**	Protein . . . . **3 g**

Vitamin A	**18 %**	Folic Acid	**10 %**
Vitamin C	**13 %**	Vitamin B12	**2 %**
Calcium	**3 %**	Pantothenic Acid	**2 %**
Iron	**7 %**	Phosphorus	**6 %**
Vitamin E	**1 %**	Magnesium	**7 %**
Vitamin K	**29 %**	Zinc	**3 %**
Vitamin B1	**4 %**	Selenium	**8 %**
Vitamin B2	**2 %**	Copper	**6 %**
Niacin	**4 %**	Manganese	**10 %**
Vitamin B6	**5 %**		

OTHER BENEFICIAL NUTRIENTS (PER SERVING)

Omega-3 (ALA+EPA+DPA+DHA) . . .	**3 mg**
Choline	**13 mg**
Beta-Carotene	**428 mcg**
Alpha-Carotene	**1 mcg**
Lutein & Zeaxanthin	**269 mcg**

TUNA SALAD ON A BED OF AVOCADO

8 SERVINGS • PREPARATION: 13 MINUTES • EASY

Tuna salad is always one of Andrew's favorite quick protein snacks and a rich source of Omega-3s. We try not to use too much mayonnaise and to instead use other ingredients to impart the best flavor, moisture, texture and mouth feel. Andrew likes it when I add some hardboiled egg white for extra protein and even more moisture. Andrew enjoys his tuna salad with avocado or guacamole, so I often simply place the tuna salad on top of an avocado half or alongside some guacamole. He also enjoys it with our Turmeric Hummus (Recipe 12), so I sometimes create a little plate for him as a snack during the day with a small dollop of each of his favorites.

4 - 6 baby carrots, finely chopped

1 stalk celery, finely chopped

1 clove garlic, finely chopped

1 small shallot, finely chopped

12 oz. can tuna

¼ cup mayonnaise

1 tbsp. Dijon mustard

1 tsp. garlic powder

1 tsp. onion powder

Juice of 1 lemon

Salt and freshly ground black pepper to taste

1 oz. chives or scallions, finely chopped

2 avocados, halved and pitted

1 Finely chop the carrots, celery, garlic and shallots in batches in a small blender or by hand. Place in a bowl and reserve.

2 In a small blender, mix the tuna, mayonnaise, mustard, garlic powder, onion powder, lemon, salt and pepper.

3 Add the tuna mixture to the vegetables, along with the chives, and mix well. Season to taste.

4 Chop the avocados into cubes and squeeze lemon juice on the top to preserve the color.

5 I prefer to use a ring mold to form the avocado and tuna salad for a nicer presentation. First add chopped avocado, then top with tuna mixture. Remove from mold and garnish with chives.

Nutrition Information

Servings **8**

Calories	**192**	Potassium	**492 mg**
Calories from fat	**106**	Total Carbohydrates	**10 g**
Total Fat	**12 g**	Dietary Fiber	**5 g**
Cholesterol	**17 mg**	Sugars	**2 g**
Sodium	**153 mg**	Protein	**12 g**
Vitamin A	**125 %**	Vitamin B6	**20 %**
Vitamin C	**17 %**	Folic Acid	**13 %**
Calcium	**3 %**	Vitamin B12	**67 %**
Iron	**5 %**	Pantothenic Acid	**13 %**
Vitamin D	**24 %**	Phosphorus	**16 %**
Vitamin E	**9 %**	Magnesium	**11 %**
Vitamin K	**5 %**	Zinc	**5 %**
Vitamin B1	**12 %**	Selenium	**25 %**
Vitamin B2	**12 %**	Copper	**8 %**
Niacin	**25 %**	Manganese	**8 %**

OTHER BENEFICIAL NUTRIENTS (PER SERVING)

Omega-3 (ALA+EPA+DPA+DHA)	**1 mg**
Choline	**40 mg**
Beta-Carotene	**2,647 mcg**
Alpha-Carotene	**1,099 mcg**
Lutein & Zeaxanthin	**235 mcg**

ASIAN TURKEY MEATBALLS
WITH SATAY SAUCE

25-30 MEATBALLS • PREPARATION: 20 MINUTES • COOKING: 13-15 MINUTES • MEDIUM

I love cooking with Asian flavors and when I was looking for a nice high-protein appetizer, I decided on creating low-calorie Asian meatballs. These are delicious and surprisingly easy to make. To eliminate wheat and gluten, I use oat bran, which provides a nice moist texture and a healthy source of fiber. I include a hint of mint for freshness and our Satay sauce is the perfect savory addition. If you decide to cook the meatballs on wood skewers, be sure to soak the skewers in water for about a half hour before cooking so they are more resistant to burning.

Meatballs:

Cooking oil spray

1 lb. ground turkey

¾ cup oat bran

1 cup mushrooms, finely chopped

2 garlic cloves, minced

1 shallot, chopped

1 oz. fresh mint, minced
   (reserve some for garnish)

1 tsp. ginger, minced or ground

1 tsp. coriander

1 tsp. fennel seeds

1 egg (or 2 egg whites)

Salt and freshly ground
   pepper to taste

A few leaves of Bibb lettuce

Peanuts for garnish

Satay Sauce:

2 tbsp. peanut or
   cashew butter

½ cup coconut milk

¼ cup lime juice

1 tbsp. agave syrup

1 tsp. curry powder

1 clove garlic, minced

½ tsp. Sriracha or
   chili flakes to taste

1 Preheat the oven to 350°. In a large bowl, mix the turkey, oat bran, mushrooms, garlic, shallot, mint, ginger, coriander, fennel seeds, egg, salt and pepper. If the mixture appears dry or doesn't easily form into balls, add an additional egg white.

2 Prepare the Satay Sauce by whisking all the ingredients in a bowl until smooth and creamy.

3 Line a baking sheet with foil and spray with cooking oil. Form mini meatballs approximately 1½ inches in diameter and place them on the sheet. Bake for 11 to 12 minutes and then broil for 2 minutes until golden.

4 Serve the meatballs on Bibb lettuce leaves garnished with mint leaves and nuts. Serve the Satay Sauce on the side.

Nutrition Information

Serving Size **1 Meatball** Servings **30**

Calories **35**	Potassium . . . . **66 mg**
Calories from fat **13**	Total Carbohydrates . . . . **2 g**
Total Fat . . . . **1 g**	Dietary Fiber . . . . **0 g**
Cholesterol . . . . . . **11 mg**	Sugars . . . . **0 g**
Sodium . . . . **15 mg**	Protein . . . . **4 g**

Vitamin A . . . . **1 %**	Vitamin B12 . . . . **3 %**
Calcium . . . . **1 %**	Pantothenic Acid . . . . **2 %**
Iron . . . . **2 %**	Phosphorus . . . . **5 %**
Vitamin D . . . . **1 %**	Magnesium . . . . **2 %**
Vitamin B1 . . . . **3 %**	Zinc . . . . **3 %**
Vitamin B2 . . . . **3 %**	Selenium . . . . **7 %**
Niacin . . . . **5 %**	Copper . . . . **2 %**
Vitamin B6 . . . . **3 %**	Manganese . . . . **8 %**
Folic Acid . . . . **1 %**	

OTHER BENEFICIAL NUTRIENTS (PER SERVING)

Omega-3 (ALA+EPA+DPA+DHA) . . **25 mg**

Choline . . . . **9 mg**

Beta-Carotene . . . . **3 mcg**

Lutein & Zeaxanthin . . . . **5 mcg**

Angelica's Favorite Date

20 SERVINGS • PREPARATION: 15 MINUTES • COOKING: 10 MINUTES • EASY

Given the name of this recipe, you might think we are talking about someone's social calendar, but we are really talking about that delicious fruit from the date palm tree. We love dates. When I moved to Australia more than 20 years ago, my roommate made these delicious "Devil on Horseback" appetizers, which were simply bacon-wrapped dates. What's not to like?! I had completely forgotten about them until recently when my girlfriend, Angelica, mentioned them to me, so I decided to create a far healthier version for everyone to enjoy.

20 large dates, pitted and halved

10 thin slices prosciutto,
    cut in half

5 ½ oz. goat, blue or Stilton cheese

1 oz. fresh chives (half for garnish),
    minced

Salt and freshly ground black
    pepper to taste

A few kale or arugula leaves

20 toothpicks soaked in
    water for 10 minutes

Thick balsamic vinegar for
    garnish

1 Preheat the oven to 400°. Line a baking sheet with tin foil. Using a fork, mix together the cheese, chives, salt and pepper in a small bowl.

2 Fill the inside of each date with approximately 1 teaspoon of the cheese mixture.

3 Roll each date in prosciutto, skewer with a toothpick and place on the lined baking sheet.

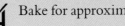

4 Bake for approximately 10 minutes.

5 Place each rolled date on a kale or arugula leaf, and garnish with chives and a drizzle of balsamic vinegar.

Nutrition Information

Serving Size **1 Date**   Servings **20**

Calories	**67**	Potassium	**108 mg**
Calories from fat	**32**	Total Carbohydrates	**7 g**
Total Fat	**4 g**	Dietary Fiber	**1 g**
Cholesterol	**14 mg**	Sugars	**5 g**
Sodium	**224 mg**	Protein	**2 g**

Vitamin A	**4 %**	Vitamin B12	**1 %**
Vitamin C	**3 %**	Pantothenic Acid	**1 %**
Calcium	**3 %**	Phosphorus	**6 %**
Iron	**2 %**	Magnesium	**2 %**
Vitamin B1	**7 %**	Zinc	**2 %**
Vitamin B2	**5 %**	Selenium	**5 %**
Niacin	**3 %**	Copper	**4 %**
Vitamin B6	**3 %**	Manganese	**115 %**

OTHER BENEFICIAL NUTRIENTS (PER SERVING)

Choline	**2 mg**
Beta-Carotene	**62 mcg**
Lutein & Zeaxanthin	**72 mcg**

"SOME LIKE IT HOT" CORN CHOWDER

12 CUPS • PREPARATION: 20 MINUTES • COOKING: 25 MINUTES • MEDIUM

Andrew has loved the corn chowder at a restaurant in Los Angeles for more than 20 years. He wanted me to make a healthy low-fat version of it and he says that I have truly succeeded, since he likes my healthy version even more than the restaurant version. You can make it "as hot or not" as you like by increasing or reducing the spices, particularly the jalapeño, cayenne and optional red chili pepper. I use fresh corn on the cob, but you can also use frozen corn. This soup is destined to become your new favorite!

4 ears corn

2 tbsp. butter

1 clove garlic, minced

1 cup red onions, chopped

1 orange pepper, chopped (1½ cups)

1 red pepper, chopped (1½ cups)

½ jalapeño pepper, sliced finely (add more if you like it hot)

1 tbsp. agave syrup

2 cups skim milk, or coconut milk

2 cups chicken broth

1 tsp. cumin

¼ tsp. cayenne pepper

Salt and freshly ground pepper to taste

½ oz. fresh cilantro

½ tsp. turmeric

1 red chili pepper, diced (optional for spicier soup)

1 Place the cleaned ears of corn in a large bowl and remove the kernels using a sharp knife. Also, remove some of the pulp and reserve.

2 In a soup pot, melt the butter over medium heat and sauté the garlic, onions and peppers for 5 minutes.

3 Add the corn and sauté for 10 additional minutes.

4 Mix in the jalapeño (and red chili pepper if using), agave, milk, broth, cumin, cayenne, salt and pepper. Bring to a boil and reduce heat. Add the cilantro and cook for an additional 10 minutes.

5 Transfer soup to a blender and pulse a few times. (This is optional if you like your soups smooth as Andrew does). Serve hot, garnished with cilantro and a bit of turmeric on the top.

Nutrition Information

Serving Size **1 Cup**   Servings **12**

Calories	92	Potassium	299 mg
Calories from fat	23	Total Carbohydrates	14 g
Total Fat	3 g	Dietary Fiber	2 g
Cholesterol	6 mg	Sugars	8 g
Sodium	134 mg	Protein	4 g

Vitamin A	28 %	Vitamin B6	9 %
Vitamin C	87 %	Folic Acid	6 %
Calcium	6 %	Vitamin B12	4 %
Iron	4 %	Pantothenic Acid	5 %
Vitamin D	2 %	Phosphorus	9 %
Vitamin E	4 %	Magnesium	9 %
Vitamin K	3 %	Zinc	3 %
Vitamin B1	7 %	Selenium	2 %
Vitamin B2	8 %	Copper	3 %
Niacin	7 %	Manganese	8 %

OTHER BENEFICIAL NUTRIENTS (PER SERVING)

Omega-3 (ALA+EPA+DPA+DHA)	8 mg
Choline	19 mg
Beta-Carotene	641 mcg
Alpha-Carotene	13 mcg
Lutein & Zeaxanthin	250 mcg

EASY-TO-DO HOMEMADE CHICKEN VEGETABLE SOUP

14 CUPS • PREPARATION: 20 MINUTES • COOKING: 45 MINUTES • MEDIUM

In our first cookbook, I included Andrew's Family Cure-All Chicken Stock, which we use quite often as a base for other recipes. Then, I realized we enjoyed our chicken soup most when I included lots of fresh veggies and diced chicken. This is the "veggie soup version" of our chicken stock. We often increase the amount of chicken or vegetables or add cooked barley or brown rice when we want a heartier version. It's great anytime as a healthy, low-calorie, protein rich snack or as part of the perfect meal when someone in the family might be under the weather.

1½ cups red onions, chopped	4 cups water	1 oz. fresh parsley
3 garlic cloves, minced	2 chicken breasts, diced	1 oz. fresh thyme
1½ cups carrots, chopped	Salt and freshly ground pepper to taste	1 cup tomato, chopped
1½ cups celery, chopped		Cooked barley or brown rice, optional
4 cups chicken broth	1 bay leaf	

1 In a large soup pot over medium heat, add the onions, garlic, carrots and celery, along with the broth and water. Cook for 5 minutes.

2 Add the diced chicken to the vegetables and broth. Bring to a boil and reduce heat. Season with salt and pepper.

3 Add the herbs to the soup and simmer on low for 30 minutes.

4 Add the chopped tomatoes and cook for an additional 10 minutes.

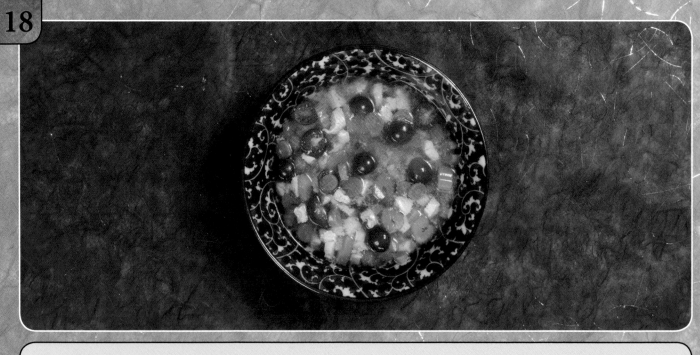

5 Remove the bay leaf and serve in a bowl as is, or with cooked barley or brown rice.

Nutrition Information

Serving Size **1 Cup** Servings **14**

Calories	**106**	Potassium	**282 mg**
Calories from fat	**60**	Total Carbohydrates	**4 g**
Total Fat	**7 g**	Dietary Fiber	**1 g**
Cholesterol	**17 mg**	Sugars	**3 g**
Sodium	**365 mg**	Protein	**8 g**

Vitamin A	**50 %**	Folic Acid	**5 %**
Vitamin C	**10 %**	Vitamin B12	**3 %**
Calcium	**3 %**	Pantothenic Acid	**5 %**
Iron	**5 %**	Phosphorus	**12 %**
Vitamin E	**1 %**	Magnesium	**4 %**
Vitamin K	**26 %**	Zinc	**3 %**
Vitamin B1	**8 %**	Selenium	**15 %**
Vitamin B2	**4 %**	Copper	**7 %**
Niacin	**16 %**	Manganese	**11 %**
Vitamin B6	**4 %**		

OTHER BENEFICIAL NUTRIENTS (PER SERVING)

Choline	**46 mg**
Beta-Carotene	**1,233 mcg**
Alpha-Carotene	**490 mcg**
Lutein & Zeaxanthin	**97 mcg**
Lycopene	**331 mcg**

SPINACH SALAD WITH STRAWBERRIES AND GOAT CHEESE

13 CUPS • PREPARATION: 15 MINUTES • COOKING: 15 MINUTES • EASY

As much as I love kale, Andrew loves his spinach, and he really likes the flavor combination with strawberries, goat cheese and this sweet and savory dressing. Our good friend Eric suggested using jicama for crunchiness, and lately, I seem to find myself adding quinoa to all sorts of things. When making the dressing, I use our Strawberry Jam (Recipe 11), but any berry or fig jam works just as well.

Salad:

2 cups cooked quinoa

1½ cups candied walnuts

1 tsp. olive oil

1 tsp. agave

4 to 5 cups packed spinach

4 cups cut strawberries

1½ cups jicama

5½ oz. goat cheese, crumbled

Dressing:

1 tbsp. balsamic vinegar

1 tbsp. old-style mustard

1 tbsp. strawberry jam

1 clove garlic, minced

⅓ cup olive oil

1 tbsp. lemon juice

A few sprigs of fresh mint

Salt and freshly ground black pepper to taste

1 Cook the quinoa according to the package directions. Typically, it is 1 cup quinoa to 2 cups of water with a pinch of salt and pepper, and a little olive oil. Bring to a boil, lower heat, and simmer for 15 minutes.

2 In a small skillet over medium heat, cook the walnuts with a drop of oil and the agave for approximately 5 minutes until they caramelize.

3 Wisk all dressing ingredients until smooth. Some jams may make it too thick and if so, add a few drops of water and continue whisking until smooth.

4 Peel and cube the jicama.

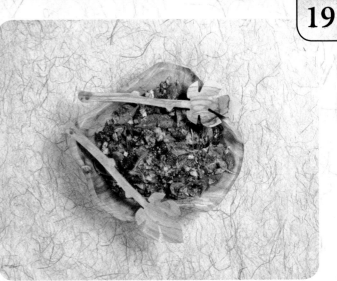

5 In a large salad bowl, add the spinach, strawberries, jicama, goat cheese, cooked quinoa and caramelized walnuts.

6 Toss the dressing with the salad, and serve.

Nutrition Information

Serving Size **1 Cup**   Servings **13**

Calories	**304**	Potassium	**392 mg**
Calories from fat	**136**	Total Carbohydrates	**37 g**
Total Fat	**15 g**	Dietary Fiber	**10 g**
Cholesterol	**10 mg**	Sugars	**13 g**
Sodium	**203 mg**	Protein	**9 g**

Vitamin A	**25 %**	Folic Acid	**21 %**
Vitamin C	**58 %**	Pantothenic Acid	**3 %**
Calcium	**9 %**	Phosphorus	**19 %**
Iron	**13 %**	Magnesium	**18 %**
Vitamin D	**1 %**	Zinc	**7 %**
Vitamin E	**5 %**	Selenium	**5 %**
Vitamin B1	**9 %**	Copper	**14 %**
Vitamin B2	**12 %**	Manganese	**210 %**
Niacin	**4 %**		
Vitamin B6	**10 %**		

OTHER BENEFICIAL NUTRIENTS (PER SERVING)

Omega-3 (ALA+EPA+DPA+DHA)	**8 mg**
Choline	**28 mg**
Beta-Carotene	**666 mcg**
Lutein & Zeaxanthin	**1,463 mcg**

DELICIOUS CHINESE CHICKEN SALAD

12 CUPS • PREPARATION: 35 MINUTES • COOKING: 15-18 MINUTES • MEDIUM

Andrew loves Chinese chicken salads because of all the cabbage they contain, but he always orders them without fried wontons, so I wanted to find him a crunchy and healthy alternative. The cashews and sesame seeds in our recipe provide a pleasant and healthy crunchiness, so you don't even miss the wontons. The dressing on this salad is always a major crowd-pleaser no matter when and where you use it.

Chicken:

4 skinless chicken breasts

1 tbsp. dark sesame oil

¼ tsp. kosher salt

¼ tsp. crushed pepper

1½ tsp. ground ginger

2 tsp. garlic powder

1 oz. scallions, chopped

Salad:

4 cups Chinese (Napa) cabbage, finely chopped

3 cups red cabbage, chopped

1 cup carrots, chopped

¼ cup scallions, thinly sliced

¼ cup sesame seeds or roasted cashews

Dressing:

¼ cup dark sesame oil

¼ cup lime juice

3 tbsp. creamy peanut butter

1 large garlic clove

Salt and freshly ground black pepper to taste

2 tbsp. agave

Sriracha, to taste

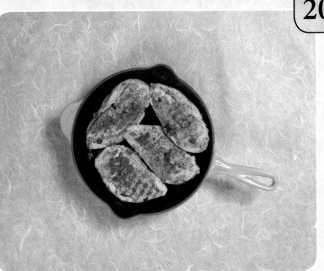

1 Preheat oven to 375° and season the chicken with salt, pepper, ginger and garlic. Heat oil in an ovenproof skillet over high heat and place chicken in the pan, immediately lowering the heat to medium. Sear the chicken for 4 minutes on each side until golden.

2 In the same skillet, bake the chicken for about 10 minutes (more for thicker breasts) until cooked through. Remove from oven, cool and sprinkle with chopped scallions.

3 Place all the dressing ingredients in a blender and process until smooth.

4 In a large bowl, mix the cabbage, carrots and scallions, and sprinkle with sesame seeds or cashews.

5 Toss the salad with half of the dressing, and top with the sliced chicken. Serve with the remaining dressing on the side.

Nutrition Information

Serving Size **1 Cup**	Servings **12**
Calories **267**	Potassium . . . . . . **339 mg**
Calories from fat . . . **168**	Total Carbohydrates . . . **14 g**
Total Fat . . . . **19 g**	Dietary Fiber . . . . **1 g**
Cholesterol . . . . . . **24 mg**	Sugars . . . . **9 g**
Sodium . . . . **360 mg**	Protein . . . . **11 g**

Vitamin A	**65 %**	Folic Acid	**13 %**
Vitamin C	**42 %**	Vitamin B12	**3 %**
Calcium	**6 %**	Pantothenic Acid	**6 %**
Iron	**11 %**	Phosphorus	**18 %**
Vitamin E.	**11 %**	Magnesium	**12 %**
Vitamin K	**48 %**	Zinc	**10 %**
Vitamin B1	**12 %**	Selenium	**23 %**
Vitamin B2	**7 %**	Copper	**16 %**
Niacin	**22 %**	Manganese	**14 %**
Vitamin B6	**13 %**		

OTHER BENEFICIAL NUTRIENTS (PER SERVING)

Choline	**69 mg**
Beta-Carotene	**1,655 mcg**
Alpha-Carotene	**371 mcg**
Lutein & Zeaxanthin	**131 mcg**
Lycopene	**4 mcg**

GREEK SALAD
WITH KALE AND WATERMELON

13 CUPS • PREPARATION: 20 MINUTES • EASY

This is my delicious version of a Greek salad, and with the addition of a healthy protein source such as a piece of grilled chicken or salmon, it becomes a complete meal. We like the mix of the black and green kale for its beautiful, healthy color, but you can see what kale is available at your supermarket. Although he knows how healthy they are, Andrew doesn't like olives, but I LOVE them, so the black Kalamata olives are optional at our household. Watermelon makes for a wonderful flavor addition to a Greek salad and its high lycopene content combined with kale's high levels of lutein and zeaxanthin make this a real "Carotenoid Salad." I chose to use fennel instead of cucumber in this recipe for a different taste twist, but either is fine.

Salad:
3 cups black kale, chopped
3 cups green kale, chopped
2 cups watermelon, cubed
1 cup fennel, sliced
1 cup chopped feta cheese
1 cup cherry tomatoes, halved

1 oz. fresh oregano
(dill is a good alternative)
½ cup black Kalamata pitted olives
(optional)

Dressing:
2 tbsp. honey mustard
Zest of 1 orange

¼ cup orange juice
2 tbsp. apple cider vinegar
1 tbsp. poppy seeds
¼ cup fat-free yogurt
1 small shallot, minced
Salt and freshly ground black
pepper to taste
¼ cup olive oil

1 In a large salad bowl, mix together all the salad ingredients.

2 Whisk together all the dressing ingredients in a small bowl.

3 Toss the salad and dressing well. Serve at the beginning of a meal, or top with a piece of grilled chicken for a main course.

Nutrition Information

Serving Size **1 Cup**   Servings **13**

Calories **139**	Potassium . . . . . . **271 mg**
Calories from fat **83**	Total Carbohydrates . . . **10 g**
Total Fat . . . . **9 g**	Dietary Fiber . . . . **4 g**
Cholesterol . . . . . . **11 mg**	Sugars . . . . **3 g**
Sodium . . . . **288 mg**	Protein . . . . **4 g**

Vitamin A . . . . **22 %**	Folic Acid. . . . . **4 %**
Vitamin C . . . . **28 %**	Vitamin B12 . . . . **4 %**
Calcium . . . . **20 %**	Pantothenic Acid . . . . **3 %**
Iron . . . . **13 %**	Phosphorus. . . . . . . **11 %**
Vitamin E. . . . . **5 %**	Magnesium. . . . . . . **12 %**
Vitamin K . . . . **65 %**	Zinc . . . . **6 %**
Vitamin B1. . . . . . . **8 %**	Selenium . . . . **8 %**
Vitamin B2. . . . . . . **9 %**	Copper. . . . . **12 %**
Niacin . . . . **4 %**	Manganese . . . . **34 %**
Vitamin B6. . . . . . . **7 %**	

OTHER BENEFICIAL NUTRIENTS (PER SERVING)

Choline.	**8 mg**
Beta-Carotene.	**589 mcg**
Alpha-Carotene	**16 mcg**
Lutein & Zeaxanthin.	**675 mcg**
Lycopene.	**295 mcg**

KOBB SALAD WITH SHRIMP

15 CUPS • PREPARATION: 30 MINUTES • COOKING: 12 MINUTES • MEDIUM

There are many restaurants we have been to that offer a delicious Maine Lobster Cobb Salad. Since lobster can be quite costly and not always available, I thought I would reinvent this Cobb salad using healthier Kale and less costly Shrimp, thus creating our Shrimp Kobb Salad. If you like, you can use the more standard blue cheese of a Cobb salad, but since Andrew does not like blue cheese, we replaced it with his favorite Jarlsberg Swiss Cheese. This dressing is another winner that you will likely find yourself using with other favorite salads at home.

Honey Mustard Tarragon Dressing:

¼ cup lemon juice

1 tbsp. white wine vinegar

1 tbsp. agave or honey

1 tbsp. coarse-grain mustard

½ cup olive oil

1 small shallot, diced

Salt and freshly ground pepper to taste

1 oz. fresh tarragon, thinly sliced

Cobb Salad:

4 slices turkey bacon

1 lb. large uncooked shrimp, peeled and deveined

Lemon pepper, to taste

Kosher salt

9 quail eggs

4 cups romaine lettuce, chopped

3 cups kale, chopped

1 cup cherry tomatoes, halved

1 cup orange pepper, diced

1 cup Jarlsberg cheese, cubed

2 avocados, sliced

7 oz. jar baby corn

1 oz. fresh tarragon, thinly sliced

1   Mix all the ingredients for the dressing, except the tarragon, in a blender or with a small whisk. Fold in the sliced tarragon at the end and set aside.

2   Cook the bacon in a large nonstick skillet over medium heat. Cut in small pieces and set aside.

3   Add the shrimp and lemon pepper to the same pan with the bacon grease and sauté over medium to high heat for approximately 3 minutes on each side (depending on their size) until done. Lightly sprinkle with salt at the end and set aside.

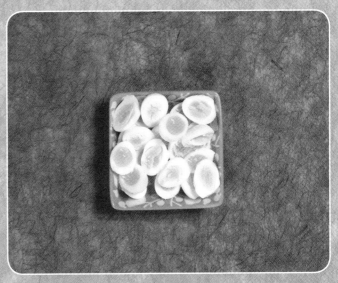

4   Boil the quail eggs in boiling water for 2-1/2 to 3 minutes. Place in bath of cold water and peel. Cut eggs in half and set aside.

5 In a large bowl, mix the lettuce, kale, tomatoes, peppers, cheese, avocado, bacon bits, eggs and corn.

6 Toss the salad with the dressing, top with the sautéed shrimp, and garnish with tarragon.

Nutrition Information

| Serving Size **1 Cup** | | Servings **15** |

Calories **228**	Potassium . . . . . . **407 mg**	
Calories from fat . . . **146**	Total Carbohydrates . . . **10 g**	
Total Fat . . . . **16 g**	Dietary Fiber . . . . **3 g**	
Cholesterol . . . . . **106 mg**	Sugars . . . . **2 g**	
Sodium . . . . **287 mg**	Protein . . . . **10 g**	

Vitamin A . . . . **37 %**	Vitamin B6. . . . . . . **14 %**
Vitamin C . . . . **20 %**	Folic Acid. . . . . **16 %**
Calcium . . . . **15 %**	Vitamin B12. . . . . . **13 %**
Iron . . . . **12 %**	Pantothenic Acid . . . . **7 %**
Vitamin D . . . . **2 %**	Phosphorus. . . . . . . **19 %**
Vitamin E. . . . . . . **11 %**	Magnesium. . . . . . . **10 %**
Vitamin K . . . . **58 %**	Zinc . . . . **9 %**
Vitamin B1. . . . . . . **5 %**	Selenium . . . . **20 %**
Vitamin B2. . . . . . **12 %**	Copper. . . . . **11 %**
Niacin . . . . **9 %**	Manganese . . . . **21 %**

OTHER BENEFICIAL NUTRIENTS (PER SERVING)

Omega-3 (ALA+EPA+DPA+DHA). .	**82 mg**
Choline.	**52 mg**
Beta-Carotene	**916 mcg**
Alpha-Carotene	**18 mcg**
Lutein & Zeaxanthin	**662 mcg**
Lycopene.	**256 mcg**

BROCCOLI SALAD WITH YELLOW RAISINS AND PINE NUTS

8 CUPS • PREPARATION: 15 MINUTES • COOKING: 5 MINUTES • EASY

Broccoli is one of our favorite cruciferous vegetables and this salad can also act as a perfect side dish for almost anything. Because the broccoli should not be over-steamed, it will be crunchy and delicious with some mild sweetness from the raisins and a bit of creaminess from the dressing. It is a delicious way to introduce more cruciferous vegetables into your diet. You can always reduce the shallots if their flavor is too strong.

Salad:

12 oz. (approx. 6 cups) broccoli florets

½ cup golden raisins

½ cup pine nuts

Dressing:

¼ cup light mayonnaise

3 tbsp. fat-free yogurt

1 small shallot, diced

1 tbsp. agave or maple syrup

1 tbsp. apple cider vinegar

½ tsp. garlic powder

½ tsp. chili flakes (optional)

Salt and freshly ground black pepper to taste

1 Steam the broccoli florets for 4–5 minutes.

2 Remove from steamer, strain and plunge into ice water to retain color.

3 Whisk together light mayo, fat-free yogurt, minced shallots, garlic powder, agave, apple cider vinegar, chili flakes and salt and pepper in a small bowl.

4 In a large salad bowl, combine the cooked broccoli, raisins, and pine nuts. Toss the salad and dressing until well mixed. Serve in individual bowls.

Nutrition Information

Serving Size 1 Cup   **Servings 8**

Calories **139**	Potassium . . . . . . **196 mg**
Calories from fat **77**	Total Carbohydrates . . . **13 g**
Total Fat . . . . **9 g**	Dietary Fiber . . . . **1 g**
Cholesterol . . . . **2 mg**	Sugars . . . . **9 g**
Sodium . . . . **80 mg**	Protein . . . . **3 g**

Vitamin A . . . . . . **2 %**	Folic Acid. . . . . **4 %**
Vitamin C . . . . **25 %**	Vitamin B12. . . . . **1 %**
Calcium . . . . **3 %**	Pantothenic Acid . . . . **2 %**
Iron . . . . **5 %**	Phosphorus. . . . . **8 %**
Vitamin E. . . . . **6 %**	Magnesium. . . . . **7 %**
Vitamin K . . . . . . **22 %**	Zinc . . . . **5 %**
Vitamin B1 . . . . **4 %**	Selenium . . . . **1 %**
Vitamin B2. . . . . . . **4 %**	Copper. . . . . **8 %**
Niacin . . . . **3 %**	Manganese . . . . **41 %**
Vitamin B6. . . . . . . **4 %**	

OTHER BENEFICIAL NUTRIENTS (PER SERVING)

Choline.	**10 mg**
Beta-Carotene.	**68 mcg**
Alpha-Carotene	**4 mcg**
Lutein & Zeaxanthin.	**242 mcg**

CHOPPED KALE CAESAR (KAESAR) SALAD WITH PARMESAN CRISPS

12 CUPS • PREPARATION: 25 MINUTES • COOKING: 13 MINUTES • MEDIUM

A classic Caesar Salad has always been my favorite salad. When I go out to lunch, I typically order a Caesar Salad without croutons, but topped with a piece of grilled salmon. The difference in our salad is that I complement the romaine lettuce with highly nutrient dense kale. By finely chopping the kale it adds a wonderful flavor and texture to the salad. For those of you who miss the croutons, you can enjoy our delicious Parmesan Crisps. At home when I make our low-calorie Chopped Kaesar Salad I generally top it with our Maple Chili Salmon (Recipe 25).

Parmesan Crisps:
Olive oil cooking spray
1 cup Parmesan cheese, grated
½ oz. fresh thyme
½ tsp. paprika

Dressing:
Juice of 2 lemons with zest
½ cup Parmesan cheese, shredded

½ cup fat-free yogurt
1 tbsp. Dijon mustard
1 garlic clove, minced
1 tsp. Worcestershire sauce
⅓ cup olive oil
Chili pepper flakes (optional)
Salt and freshly ground black pepper to taste

1 oz. fresh thyme

Salad:
6½ cups romaine lettuce, chopped
3 cups kale, chopped
1 cup Parmesan cheese, shredded
½ cup roasted pine nuts

1   Preheat the oven to 450°. Line a baking sheet with tin foil and spray with olive oil. Arrange 1 tsp. sprinkles of Parmesan cheese on the baking sheet topping each with a little thyme and paprika.

2   Bake for approximately 3 minutes until crisp. Remove carefully with a soft spatula and set aside to cool.

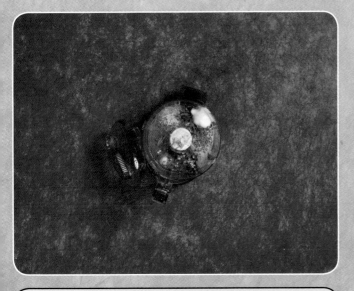

3   Mix all the dressing ingredients in a mini blender or whisk them in a medium bowl until smooth.

4   In a large salad bowl, add the romaine, kale, Parmesan cheese and pine nuts.

5 Toss with the dressing and top with the Parmesan crisps.

Nutrition Information

Serving Size **1 Cup**   Servings **12**

Calories	143	Potassium	166 mg
Calories from fat	110	Total Carbohydrates	4 g
Total Fat	12 g	Dietary Fiber	1 g
Cholesterol	6 mg	Sugars	1 g
Sodium	156 mg	Protein	4 g

Vitamin A	55 %	Vitamin B12	2 %
Vitamin C	20 %	Pantothenic Acid	2 %
Calcium	12 %	Phosphorus	11 %
Iron	5 %	Magnesium	7 %
Vitamin E	8 %	Zinc	5 %
Vitamin B1	4 %	Selenium	4 %
Vitamin B2	5 %	Copper	8 %
Niacin	2 %	Manganese	30 %
Vitamin B6	3 %		
Folic Acid	10 %		

OTHER BENEFICIAL NUTRIENTS (PER SERVING)

Omega-3 (ALA+EPA+DPA+DHA)	63 mg
Choline	9 mg
Beta-Carotene	1,619 mcg
Alpha-Carotene	3 mcg
Lutein & Zeaxanthin	938 mcg

MAPLE CHILI SALMON

4 SERVINGS • PREPARATION: 5 MINUTES • COOKING: 12 MINUTES • MEDIUM

This salmon is so simple yet so flavorful. All you do is start with the best fresh salmon filets you can find. I prefer to use wild salmon, but I suppose farmed salmon is better than nothing, as long as it is fresh and of high quality. As I mentioned previously, I use this salmon as my standard topping for my Chopped Kale Kaesar Salad (Recipe 24). We don't like our salmon cooked through. I guess you can call it "medium rare," since we only broil it for about eight minutes. You can leave it under the broiler for a few more minutes until it meets your preference. Also, I sometimes add Ancho chilies to the marinade for an extra flavor boost.

Cooking oil spray	1 tsp. kosher salt	1½ tsp. chili powder
4 - 4 oz. filets of wild salmon, deboned	1½ tsp. paprika	3 tbsp. maple syrup
	½ tsp. cumin	

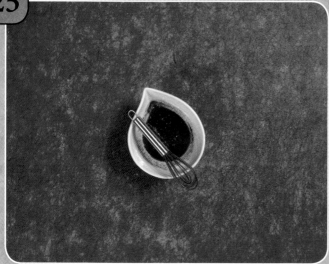

1 Preheat the broiler. Line a baking sheet with tin foil and cooking spray. Wisk together the salt, paprika, cumin, chili powder and maple syrup in a small bowl.

2 Rinse salmon filets under cold water and pat dry with paper towel. Generously brush the salmon filets with the marinade.

3 Broil salmon for approximately 8 minutes until golden and crispy. For well-done filet, brush a second time and broil 2 additional minutes.

4 Serve immediately with a drizzle of additional marinade. We like to serve it with our Chopped Kale (Kaesar) Salad with Parmesan Crisps (Recipe 24)!

Nutrition Information

Serving Size **1 Filet**   Servings **4**

Calories **176**	Potassium . . . . . . **274 mg**	
Calories from fat **48**	Total Carbohydrates . . . **11 g**	
Total Fat . . . . **5 g**	Dietary Fiber . . . . **1 g**	
Cholesterol . . . . . . **26 mg**	Sugars . . . . **10 g**	
Sodium . . . . . . **1,490 mg**	Protein . . . . **21 g**	

Vitamin A . . . . **17 %**	Vitamin B12 . . . . . . **62 %**
Calcium . . . . **4 %**	Pantothenic Acid . . . **10 %**
Iron . . . . **8 %**	Phosphorus . . . . **19 %**
Vitamin D . . . . . . **194 %**	Magnesium . . . . **7 %**
Vitamin E . . . . **9 %**	Zinc . . . . **4 %**
Vitamin B1 . . . . **3 %**	Selenium . . . . **53 %**
Vitamin B2 . . . . . . **19 %**	Copper . . . . **14 %**
Niacin . . . . **28 %**	Manganese . . . . **25 %**
Vitamin B6 . . . . **18 %**	
Folic Acid . . . . **1 %**	

OTHER BENEFICIAL NUTRIENTS (PER SERVING)

Omega-3 (ALA+EPA+DPA+DHA)	**593 mg**
Choline	**102 mg**
Beta-Carotene	**380 mcg**
Alpha-Carotene	**26 mcg**
Lutein & Zeaxanthin	**168 mcg**

TUNA BURGERS ON MUSHROOMS

10 BURGERS • PREPARATION: 30 MINUTES • COOKING: 18 MINUTES • MEDIUM

Since I am not a frequent red-meat eater, this is absolutely my favorite burger! It's so healthy, high in protein and rich in Omega-3s. The greatest challenge is finding high quality, fresh raw tuna steak, which also has a downside since it can be expensive. The cucumber salad garnish is light and refreshing and I like to use Shiitake or Portobello mushrooms as the buns. You can find what size burger works for you, but I like to use two tuna patties for each serving since they are small.

Dressing:

3 tbsp. light mayonnaise

3 tbsp. fat-free yogurt

Zest and juice of 1 lime

Salt and freshly ground black
    pepper to taste

Cucumber Salad:

2 mini cucumbers, sliced (2 cups)

½ red onion, sliced

1 tsp. agave

4 tbsp. rice vinegar

Salt and freshly ground black
    pepper to taste

Burgers:

2 lbs. tuna steak

1 clove garlic, minced

1½ tsp. fresh ginger, grated

2 tbsp. soy sauce

1 egg

½ cup oat bran

½ cup scallions, minced

1 tsp. chili flakes, optional

1 tbsp. sesame oil

20 large mushrooms
    (Portobello or Shiitake)

1 In a small bowl, mix together the mayonnaise, yogurt, lime zest and juice, and salt and pepper. Cover and chill in the refrigerator.

2 Toss together the cucumber, onion, agave, rice vinegar, and salt and pepper. Cover and chill in the refrigerator.

3 Place the tuna steak, ginger and garlic in a food processor, and pulse until finely chopped. Transfer to large mixing bowl.

4 Add the soy sauce, egg, oat bran, scallions and chili flakes. (No salt is needed due to the soy sauce.)

5 With your hands, form 10 small tuna patties. (Moisten your hands or wear plastic gloves). Add sesame oil to a skillet over medium heat and cook the tuna patties in batches for approximately 4 minutes on each side.

6 In the same skillet, heat sesame oil over medium heat. Salt and pepper the mushrooms, and cook them for approximately 4 minutes on each side.

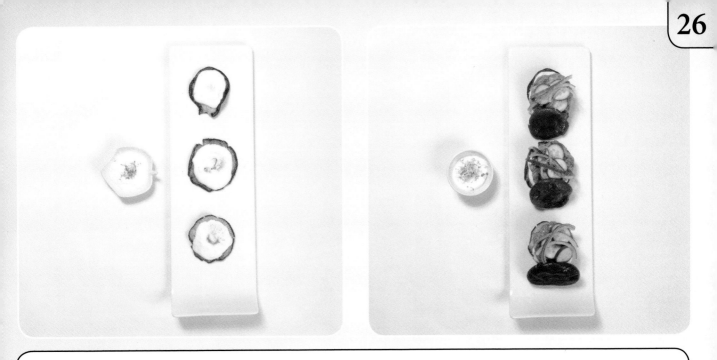

7 Assemble your burger starting with a mushroom, then sauce, tuna patties, cucumber salad, and finally top with a second mushroom.

Nutrition Information

Serving Size **1 Burger**   Servings **10**

Calories	218	Potassium	511 mg
Calories from fat	78	Total Carbohydrates	11 g
Total Fat	9 g	Dietary Fiber	2 g
Cholesterol	54 mg	Sugars	3 g
Sodium	194 mg	Protein	24 g

Vitamin A	43 %	Vitamin B6	29 %
Vitamin C	7 %	Folic Acid	5 %
Calcium	4 %	Vitamin B12	144 %
Iron	10 %	Pantothenic Acid	19 %
Vitamin D	54 %	Phosphorus	35 %
Vitamin E	6 %	Magnesium	19 %
Vitamin K	18 %	Zinc	9 %
Vitamin B1	20 %	Selenium	53 %
Vitamin B2	23 %	Copper	7 %
Niacin	48 %	Manganese	23 %

OTHER BENEFICIAL NUTRIENTS (PER SERVING)

Omega-3 (ALA+EPA+DPA+DHA)	1256 mg
Choline	81 mg
Beta-Carotene	65 mcg
Alpha-Carotene	7 mcg
Lutein & Zeaxanthin	114 mcg

FAUX-FRIED CHICKEN
WITH WALNUTS AND THYME

4 PIECES • PREPARATION: 15 MINUTES • COOKING: 15 MINUTES • MEDIUM

Since childhood, Andrew has always loved his fried chicken, but like so many of us, we were looking for a recipe that was baked rather than fried and avoided the use of breadcrumbs. This is an extremely versatile recipe that will stimulate your creativity. I sometimes replace the fat-free yogurt with low-fat buttermilk, or I use macadamia nuts instead of walnuts, or replace the corn meal with cornflake crumbs. It is easy to adapt to your tastes and requirements, but no matter how you make it, you will find it to be delicious and best of all, healthy.

4 chicken cutlets (pounded thin)

Salt and freshly ground black
    pepper to taste

1 oz. fresh thyme (reserve some
    for garnish)

Olive oil cooking spray

½ cup fat-free yogurt or
    low-fat buttermilk

2 tbsp. Dijon mustard

½ cup walnuts, chopped

½ cup cornmeal (fine) or
    cornflake crumbs.

1 tbsp. Parmesan cheese,
    finely grated

1 tsp. paprika

1 Preheat oven to 425°. Line a baking sheet with tin foil and spray with cooking oil. Season the chicken with salt and pepper, and the fresh thyme.

2 Combine the yogurt and mustard, and place the chicken in it to marinate. (This can also marinate in the refrigerator for up to 4 hours.)

3 Chop the walnuts in a blender or food processor until very fine. Then roast the walnuts and cornmeal or cornflakes in a small skillet over medium heat for 3 minutes until golden and dry.

4 On a large plate, blend the Parmesan cheese, walnuts, cornmeal and paprika.

5 Take each chicken cutlet from the yogurt mixture and dip in the walnut mixture turning until well coated. Place on the lined baking sheet, lightly sprayed with cooking oil.

6 Bake for 15 minutes or until desired doneness. Serve garnished with fresh thyme.

Nutrition Information

Serving Size **1/2 Breast**   Servings **8**

Calories **211**	Potassium . . . . . . **521 mg**
Calories from fat **63**	Total Carbohydrates . . . . **5 g**
Total Fat . . . . **7 g**	Dietary Fiber . . . . **1 g**
Cholesterol . . . . . **102 mg**	Sugars . . . . **1 g**
Sodium . . . . **123 mg**	Protein . . . . **32 g**

Vitamin A . . . . **5 %**	Folic Acid. . . . . **5 %**
Vitamin C . . . . **2 %**	Vitamin B12. . . . . . . **2 %**
Calcium . . . . **4 %**	Pantothenic Acid . . . **22 %**
Iron . . . . **5 %**	Phosphorus. . . . . . . **34 %**
Vitamin E. . . . . **5 %**	Magnesium. . . . . . . **14 %**
Vitamin K . . . . **1 %**	Zinc . . . . **8 %**
Vitamin B1. . . . . . **12 %**	Selenium . . . . **48 %**
Vitamin B2. . . . . . **17 %**	Copper. . . . . **6 %**
Niacin . . . . **67 %**	Manganese . . . . **10 %**
Vitamin B6. . . . . . **58 %**	

OTHER BENEFICIAL NUTRIENTS (PER SERVING)

Omega-3 (ALA+EPA+DPA+DHA) . . **53 mg**	
Choline . . . . **117 mg**	
Beta-Carotene. . . . . **99 mcg**	
Alpha-Carotene . . . . **4 mcg**	
Lutein & Zeaxanthin. . . . . **107 mcg**	

OUR SWEET AND SOUR CHICKEN

12 CUPS • PREPARATION: 25 MINUTES • COOKING: 25 MINUTES • MEDIUM

As a child growing up in an international city like Paris, I experienced a wide variety of Asian cuisine. Despite my very "French" training at Le Cordon Bleu, my love for Asian flavors and spices has remained. Andrew grew up in New York where a visit to Chinatown was always a treat and he loved Sweet and Sour Chicken. My version of this favorite is a perfect example of how well Asian flavors and spices complement the healthy foods we love. The lean chicken with the healthy red and orange peppers, along with pineapple make this as delicious as it is healthy and easy to make. You can also serve it over brown rice with a side of sautéed snow peas.

1 tbsp. sesame oil

4 skinless chicken breasts, cubed
    into 1½ inch pieces

Salt and freshly ground black
    pepper to taste

1 tsp. ground ginger

¾ cup red pepper

¾ cup orange pepper

¾ cup yellow pepper

1 medium red onion, chopped

2 garlic cloves, minced

⅓ cup low-sodium soy sauce

1 tbsp. agave or honey

3 tbsp. rice wine vinegar

¼ to ½ cup chicken broth

2 tbsp. cornstarch

1½ cups pineapple, diced

½ cup roasted cashews

1 Warm sesame oil in a large, nonstick skillet over medium to high heat and sauté the chicken, salt, pepper and ginger for approximately 5 to 7 minutes. Set aside.

2 Add the peppers, onions and garlic to the same skillet over medium heat and sauté for 5 minutes.

3 In a bowl, whisk together the soy sauce, agave, vinegar, broth and cornstarch. Add to the sautéed vegetables and mix well.

4 Add the sautéed chicken and pineapple, and simmer for an additional 8 to 10 minutes until the sauce thickens and is a nice, golden color.

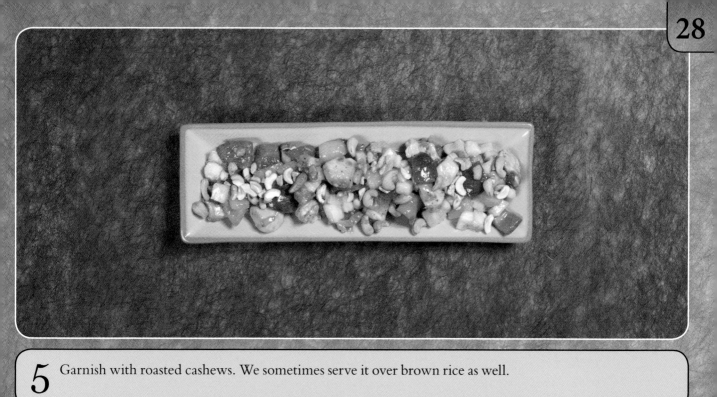

5 Garnish with roasted cashews. We sometimes serve it over brown rice as well.

Nutrition Information

Serving Size **1 Cup**   Servings **12**

Calories **211**	Potassium . . . . . . **477 mg**
Calories from fat **72**	Total Carbohydrates . . . **12 g**
Total Fat . . . . **8 g**	Dietary Fiber . . . . **1 g**
Cholesterol . . . . . . **66 mg**	Sugars . . . . **5 g**
Sodium . . . . **301 mg**	Protein . . . . **23 g**

Vitamin A . . . . **13 %**	Vitamin B12 . . . . **1 %**
Vitamin C . . . . **86 %**	Pantothenic Acid . . . **16 %**
Calcium . . . . **2 %**	Phosphorus . . . . **26 %**
Iron . . . . **7 %**	Magnesium . . . . **15 %**
Vitamin E . . . . **5 %**	Zinc . . . . **9 %**
Vitamin B1 . . . . **9 %**	Selenium . . . . **32 %**
Vitamin B2 . . . . **13 %**	Copper . . . . **15 %**
Niacin . . . . **48 %**	Manganese . . . . **19 %**
Vitamin B6 . . . . **44 %**	
Folic Acid . . . . **8 %**	

OTHER BENEFICIAL NUTRIENTS (PER SERVING)

Omega-3 (ALA+EPA+DPA+DHA) . . **24 mg**

Choline . . . . **86 mg**

Beta-Carotene . . . . **322 mcg**

Alpha-Carotene . . . . **4 mcg**

Lutein & Zeaxanthin . . . . **12 mcg**

EASY COQ AU VIN (CHICKEN IN WINE SAUCE)

6 SERVINGS • PREPARATION: 30 MINUTES • COOKING: 60 MINUTES • MEDIUM

When Andrew was a child, his Mom was a big fan of the chef, Julia Child. In fact, his Mom even gave me her autographed copy of Julia Child's original cookbook! When Andrew was young, his Mom made many of Julia's traditional French dishes, including her delicious Coq au Vin. As a result, Andrew shares my love for this very traditional French dish. Our Coq au Vin is easy to prepare and wonderfully rich in flavor. Some folks prefer white wine, but we generally use red wine, because of its richer flavor and higher content of protective compounds. Of course, all the alcohol evaporates when you cook the dish. In France, this dish is traditionally served with potatoes, but since we rarely eat potatoes, we replaced them with carrots.

6 cups (1½ lbs.) carrots

1 (5 lbs.) whole organic chicken, cut in parts

Salt and freshly ground black pepper to taste

4 slices turkey bacon, minced

1 tbsp. butter

1 medium yellow onion, chopped

3 cloves garlic, minced

3 tbsp. oat flour

2 tbsp. tomato paste

1½ cups red wine

1 cup chicken broth

1 bay leaf

1 oz. fresh thyme (reserve a little for garnish)

1 oz. fresh marjoram (reserve a little for garnish)

1½ cups small mushrooms

1 Preheat the oven to 350°. In a steamer basket over boiling water, cook the carrots for 10 minutes. Reserve.

2 Season the chicken with salt and pepper, and a little thyme and marjoram.

3 Sauté the bacon in a Dutch oven over medium to high heat for approximately 5 minutes until crisp. Remove the bacon bits and set aside. Pour out any extra bacon grease.

4 Add butter to the Dutch oven and sauté the chicken over medium to high heat for approximately 4 minutes on each side until golden brown. Remove the chicken and set aside.

5 In the same Dutch oven, sauté the onion and garlic for 3 to 5 minutes until translucent.

6 Add the flour and tomato paste, reduce the heat, and cook approximately 5 additional minutes until it forms a roux.

7 Add the wine, broth, bay leaf, thyme and marjoram. Bring to a boil and reduce the heat to low.

8 Add the sautéed chicken and bacon to the wine broth. Cover and bake for 10 minutes.

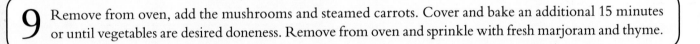

9 Remove from oven, add the mushrooms and steamed carrots. Cover and bake an additional 15 minutes or until vegetables are desired doneness. Remove from oven and sprinkle with fresh marjoram and thyme.

Nutrition Information

Servings **6**

Calories	**361**	Potassium	**1,172 mg**
Calories from fat	**209**	Total Carbohydrates	**20 g**
Total Fat	**23 g**	Dietary Fiber	**5 g**
Cholesterol	**260 mg**	Sugars	**8 g**
Sodium	**534 mg**	Protein	**48 g**

Vitamin A	**432 %**	Vitamin B6	**52 %**
Vitamin C	**19 %**	Folic Acid	**10 %**
Calcium	**11 %**	Vitamin B12	**16 %**
Iron	**18 %**	Pantothenic Acid	**29 %**
Vitamin D	**1 %**	Phosphorus	**51 %**
Vitamin E	**7 %**	Magnesium	**20 %**
Vitamin K	**34 %**	Zinc	**36 %**
Vitamin B1	**21 %**	Selenium	**81 %**
Vitamin B2	**33 %**	Copper	**18 %**
Niacin	**66 %**	Manganese	**29 %**

OTHER BENEFICIAL NUTRIENTS (PER SERVING)

Omega-3 (ALA+EPA+DPA+DHA)	**234 mg**
Choline	**151 mg**
Beta-Carotene	**10,664 mcg**
Alpha-Carotene	**4,451 mcg**
Lutein & Zeaxanthin	**371 mcg**
Lycopene	**140 mcg**

ANDREW'S MEXICAN-STYLE CHICKEN BOWL

4 SERVINGS • PREPARATION: 40 MINUTES • COOKING: 15 MINUTES • MEDIUM

Andrew had long ago created his own special bowl (no tortilla) at our local Mexican restaurant. As usual, I set out to create my own version for him at the house. This hearty, protein-rich bowl is Andrew's favorite after a hard workout. At first, I thought about adding salad, but to Andrew this bowl is more about healthy protein and fats, than salad and greens. Between the lean chicken, black beans, avocado, tomatoes and spices this is an amazing combination of foods and flavors. I think Andrew would eat it every day for lunch if we let him. Jesusita, our sous chef, even shared her special recipe for Pico de Gallo with us. You can also choose to add brown rice and garnish with lean shredded cheese and sour cream, if you wish.

Guacamole:
2 ripe avocados, peeled and pitted
¼ white onion, chopped
3 cloves garlic, crushed
½ jalapeño pepper, chopped
Juice of 1 lime
1 oz. fresh cilantro, chopped

Jesusita's Pico de Gallo:
10 oz. cherry tomatoes, chopped
3 scallions, chopped

½ jalapeño, chopped
½ white onion, chopped
Juice of 1 lime
Salt and freshly ground black
    pepper to taste
1 oz. fresh cilantro

Chicken:
2 skinless, organic chicken breasts
2 tsp. garlic powder
2 tsp. Ancho chili pepper powder

1 tsp. paprika
2 tsp. chili powder
Salt and freshly ground black
    pepper to taste
1 tsp. chili flakes (optional)
1 tsp. olive oil

Beans:
¼ white onion
1 garlic clove
15 oz. can black beans

1 Mash all the guacamole ingredients together with a fork. Cover with plastic wrap and chill in the refrigerator.

2 Mix all the Pico de Gallo ingredients together, cover and chill.

3 Season the chicken breasts with half of all the spices: garlic powder, Ancho chili pepper, paprika, chili powder, salt and pepper. Add a little olive oil to a skillet over medium to high heat and brown the chicken breasts for approximately 4 minutes on each side until golden.

4 Remove the chicken from the pan and cube it. Then return it to the pan over medium to low heat, seasoning with the remaining spices. Cook thoroughly for another 4 minutes.

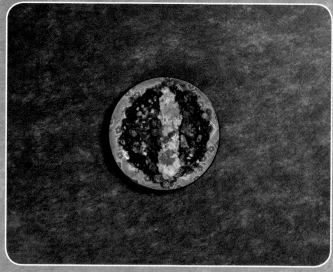

5 In a small saucepan over medium heat, combine all the bean ingredients and cook for 5 minutes until hot. (I usually cook the beans at the same time as the chicken.)

6 Assemble the dish by layering beans, Pico de Gallo, chicken, and then top with guacamole. You can also garnish with shredded cheese and sour cream, if you wish.

Nutrition Information

Servings **4**

Calories	**409**	Potassium	**1,230 mg**
Calories from fat	**194**	Total Carbohydrates	**19 g**
Total Fat	**22 g**	Dietary Fiber	**9 g**
Cholesterol	**99 mg**	Sugars	**5 g**
Sodium	**127 mg**	Protein	**34 g**
Vitamin A	**25 %**	Folic Acid	**29 %**
Vitamin C	**96 %**	Vitamin B12	**1 %**
Calcium	**4 %**	Pantothenic Acid	**37 %**
Iron	**9 %**	Phosphorus	**38 %**
Vitamin E	**22 %**	Magnesium	**21 %**
Vitamin K	**43 %**	Zinc	**12 %**
Vitamin B1	**17 %**	Selenium	**46 %**
Vitamin B2	**25 %**	Copper	**16 %**
Niacin	**78 %**	Manganese	**17 %**
Vitamin B6	**81 %**		

OTHER BENEFICIAL NUTRIENTS (PER SERVING)

Omega-3 (ALA+EPA+DPA+DHA)	**169 mg**
Choline	**136 mg**
Beta-Carotene	**618 mcg**
Alpha-Carotene	**93 mcg**
Lutein & Zeaxanthin	**679 mcg**
Lycopene	**1,198 mcg**

Sloppy Joes on Cauliflower

8 SERVINGS • PREPARATION: 20 MINUTES • COOKING: 31 MINUTES • MEDIUM

As a child, Andrew loved his Sloppy Joes. I can't say this was a recipe we covered at the Cordon Bleu in Paris, but I quickly discovered these tasty treats once I moved to America. Like so many popular dishes, they can include too much of certain unhealthy ingredients, so I made a few changes. I replaced the beef with bison and I used cauliflower instead of a bun and then I added more veggies and some delicious protective spices. You can also use grilled Portobello mushrooms to replace the bun. It is still one of Andrew's favorites.

Olive oil cooking spray

1 whole cauliflower, thinly sliced

Salt and freshly ground black
    pepper to taste

1 cup carrots, grated

1 lb. ground bison

¾ cup red onion, chopped

2 garlic cloves, minced

1 cup celery, chopped

1 tsp. cinnamon

1 tbsp. oregano

1 tsp. cumin

1 tsp. paprika

½ cup ketchup

15 oz. can diced tomatoes

1 tbsp. Dijon mustard

½ cup broth, if desired
    (beef or vegetable)

Bibb or Butter lettuce leaves

1 Preheat the oven to 375° and line a baking sheet with tin foil, spraying with olive oil. Spread the cauliflower slices on the baking sheet, and sprinkle with salt and pepper. Spray a little more cooking oil on top and bake for 15 minutes.

2 Coat a large, nonstick skillet with olive oil cooking spray. Add the carrots and bison, and brown for 5 minutes.

3 Reduce the heat to medium and add the onion, garlic, celery, cinnamon, oregano, cumin and paprika. Cook for approximately 1 minute.

4 Add the ketchup, diced tomatoes, mustard, and salt and pepper to taste. Let it all simmer over a low heat for 10 minutes. Stir in broth until sauce is desired consistency.

5 Prepare your plates by layering cauliflower slices and then lettuce leaves topped with ½ cup each of the Sloppy Joe mixture.

Nutrition Information

Serving Size **1 Sloppy Joe**   Servings **8**

Calories	**131**	Potassium	**555 mg**
Calories from fat	**42**	Total Carbohydrates	**9 g**
Total Fat	**5 g**	Dietary Fiber	**2 g**
Cholesterol	**31 mg**	Sugars	**3 g**
Sodium	**161 mg**	Protein	**14 g**

Vitamin A	**31 %**	Folic Acid	**14 %**
Vitamin C	**66 %**	Vitamin B12	**18 %**
Calcium	**7 %**	Pantothenic Acid	**6 %**
Iron	**15 %**	Phosphorus	**16 %**
Vitamin E	**3 %**	Magnesium	**9 %**
Vitamin K	**14 %**	Zinc	**20 %**
Vitamin B1	**10 %**	Selenium	**18 %**
Vitamin B2	**14 %**	Copper	**8 %**
Niacin	**19 %**	Manganese	**15 %**
Vitamin B6	**22 %**		

OTHER BENEFICIAL NUTRIENTS (PER SERVING)

Omega-3 (ALA+EPA+DPA+DHA)	**14 mg**
Choline	**86 mg**
Beta-Carotene	**769 mcg**
Alpha-Carotene	**267 mcg**
Lutein & Zeaxanthin	**150 mcg**
Lycopene	**657 mcg**

SPAGHETTI SQUASH
WITH BISON MEATBALLS

8 CUPS • PREP: 35 MINUTES • COOKING: 50 MINS. FOR SQUASH, 20 MINS. FOR MEATBALLS • MEDIUM

Who doesn't like spaghetti and meatballs? I chose to make my meatballs from bison, because it is so lean and it is now Andrew's (and Lincoln's) favorite red meat. Of course, you can choose to use ground turkey, chicken, beef, lamb or any combination that works for you. I do not add any bread, but instead use oat bran to keep them moist and add healthy fiber. I often serve these meatballs as appetizers and they just disappear. Since we do not typically eat pasta, spaghetti squash is the perfect substitute. We use our own Tomato Marinara Sauce (Recipe 33) or Rao's bottled tomato sauce from one of Andrew's old childhood favorite restaurants in New York.

The Spaghetti:

1 spaghetti squash (approx. 3 lbs.), halved lengthwise and seeded

Olive oil cooking spray

1 oz. fresh oregano

Salt and freshly ground black pepper to taste

15 oz. marinara sauce

The Meatballs:

1 lb. ground bison

½ cup Parmesan cheese, shredded + ¼ cup for garnish (optional)

2 cloves garlic, minced

1 shallot, minced

½ cup oat bran

1 egg

½ cup ketchup or marinara sauce

1 oz. fresh oregano

Salt and freshly ground black pepper to taste

1 oz. red hot chili flakes (optional)

1 Preheat oven to 400°. Lightly spray the inside of each half of the spaghetti squash with olive oil, season with oregano, salt and pepper. Place cut sides down in a pan and bake for 25 minutes. Turn squash over and bake 25 minutes longer.

2 Remove from oven and separate the strands of squash with a fork.

3 In a large bowl, mix the bison, ½ cup Parmesan cheese, garlic, shallot, oat bran, egg, ketchup or marinara, oregano, salt and pepper. Add chili flakes to taste. Mix the whole thing with your hands.

4 Form into 1-inch balls – approximately 20 to 24 depending on the size. Arrange on a baking sheet lined with tin foil and bake at 350° for 13 minutes.

5 In a saucepan over low to medium heat, bring the marinara sauce to a simmer and add the meatballs, cooking for an additional 5 minutes.

6 Serve in individual bowls. Top the spaghetti squash with marinara sauce and meatballs. Garnish with Parmesan cheese if desired.

Nutrition Information

Serving Size **1 Cup**   Servings **8**

Calories	**201**	Potassium	**448 mg**
Calories from fat	**76**	Total Carbohydrates	**14 g**
Total Fat	**8 g**	Dietary Fiber	**4 g**
Cholesterol	**59 mg**	Sugars	**4 g**
Sodium	**364 mg**	Protein	**17 g**
Vitamin A	**9 %**	Vitamin B6	**20 %**
Vitamin C	**5 %**	Folic Acid	**6 %**
Calcium	**13 %**	Vitamin B12	**20 %**
Iron	**18 %**	Pantothenic Acid	**5 %**
Vitamin D	**1 %**	Phosphorus	**23 %**
Vitamin E	**7 %**	Magnesium	**12 %**
Vitamin K	**21 %**	Zinc	**22 %**
Vitamin B1	**13 %**	Selenium	**26 %**
Vitamin B2	**15 %**	Copper	**9 %**
Niacin	**26 %**	Manganese	**29 %**

OTHER BENEFICIAL NUTRIENTS (PER SERVING)

Omega-3 (ALA+EPA+DPA+DHA)	**50 mg**
Choline	**81 mg**
Beta-Carotene	**198 mcg**
Alpha-Carotene	**12 mcg**
Lutein & Zeaxanthin	**137 mcg**
Lycopene	**4,179 mcg**

TOMATO MARINARA SAUCE

4 CUPS • PREPARATION: 15 MINUTES • COOKING: 20 MINUTES • MEDIUM

This simple sauce is a classic low-calorie staple of the healthy Mediterranean diet and Andrew loves it. I often find him eating it like a soup or using it as a dip or condiment with almost anything he eats. It can of course be used for pasta, but since we do not eat pasta, we use it as a nutritious, low-calorie alternative to catsup, mustard, mayonnaise or high-calorie sauces or dressings. It is rich in lycopene and perfect for use with our Spaghetti Squash (Recipe 32).

4 or 5 (2 lbs.) large, ripe tomatoes	3 garlic cloves, minced
1 can (14.5 oz) tomatoes, diced	1 oz. fresh basil
3 tbsp. olive oil	1 tsp. agave or honey
2 shallots, minced	Salt and freshly ground black pepper to taste

1 In a small saucepan, bring water to a boil. Plant a fork in each tomato and soak in the boiling water for 2 minutes.

2 Peel with a knife. The skin should come off effortlessly.

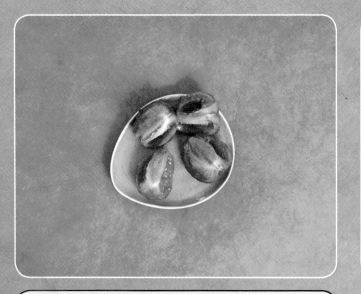

3 Cut the tomatoes in quarters and remove the seeds with a spoon.

4 In a large saucepan over medium heat, add the olive oil and sauté the garlic and shallots for one minute.

5 Combine the peeled and seeded tomatoes, the can of diced tomatoes, salt and pepper, and the agave. Cook for 15 minutes until the tomatoes are dark red.

6 Pour everything in the blender 1 to 2 minutes. Add the basil at the basil is usually minced very finely.

Nutrition Information

Serving Size **1 tbsp.**   Servings **64**

Calories **10**	Potassium . . . . **49 mg**
Calories from fat **6**	Total Carbohydrates . . . . **1 g**
Total Fat . . . . **1 g**	Dietary Fiber . . . . **0 g**
Cholesterol . . . . **0 mg**	Sugars . . . . **1 g**
Sodium . . . . **1 mg**	Protein . . . . **0 g**

Vitamin A . . . . **3 %**	Vitamin B6 . . . . **1 %**
Vitamin C . . . . **4 %**	Folic Acid . . . . **1 %**
Iron . . . . **1 %**	Phosphorus . . . . **1 %**
Vitamin E . . . . **1 %**	Magnesium . . . . **1 %**
Vitamin K . . . . **4 %**	Copper . . . . **1 %**
Vitamin B1 . . . . **1 %**	Manganese . . . . **1 %**
Niacin . . . . **1 %**	

OTHER BENEFICIAL NUTRIENTS (PER SERVING)

Choline	**2 mg**
Beta-Carotene	**82 mcg**
Alpha-Carotene	**14 mcg**
Lutein & Zeaxanthin	**48 mcg**
Lycopene	**543 mcg**

HEARTY TURKEY CHILI

13 – 14 CUPS • PREPARATION: 15 MINUTES • COOKING: 1 HOUR • EASY

This incredibly rich and hearty source of protein and fiber is Andrew's post-workout favorite. This wonderful chili can be made in advance and refrigerated up to two days. It is also delicious served over brown rice.

2 tbsp olive oil

1 medium red onion, chopped (reserve a little for garnish)

1 cup chopped green pepper

1 cup chopped red pepper

4 garlic cloves, minced

1 tbsp cumin

1 tbsp red-hot chili pepper flakes

2 to 4 tbsp chili powder, depending on heat preference

1 pack (10 oz) cherry tomatoes, halved

1 can (14.5 oz) diced tomatoes

2 tbsp tomato paste

1 can (15 oz) kidney beans, rinsed

2 cans (15 oz ea.) black beans, rinsed

1½ cups chicken broth

1 tsp dry oregano

4 cups ground or shredded turkey meat, cooked

1 tbsp salt

1 pinch ground pepper

6 oz white Cheddar cheese, shredded (optional)

1 cup Crème Fraiche (optional)

1   In a 4 to 6 quart soup pot over medium heat, warm olive oil and add onion and peppers, stirring until golden in color.

2   Add garlic, cumin, chili powder and red pepper flakes cooking for an additional 2 minutes.

3 Add tomatoes (both fresh and canned), tomato paste, broth, rinsed beans, oregano, turkey, salt and pepper, and bring to a boil. Reduce heat to low and simmer for an hour.

4 Ladle into individual bowls garnishing with shredded cheese and Crème Fraiche.

Nutrition Information

Serving Size **1 Cup**   Servings **14**

Calories **195**	Potassium . . . . . **265 mg**
Calories from fat . . **55**	Total Carbohydrates **22 g**
Total Fat . . . . **6 g**	Dietary Fiber . . . . . **9 g**
Cholesterol . . . . **26 mg**	Sugars . . . . **2 g**
Sodium . . . . **110 mg**	Protein . . . . **13 g**

Vitamin A . . . . **22 %**	Vitamin B2. . . . **17 %**	Phosphorus. . . . . **9 %**
Vitamin C . . . . **89 %**	Niacin . . . . **19 %**	Magnesium. . . . **13 %**
Calcium . . . . **4 %**	Vitamin B6. . . . **17 %**	Zinc . . . . **11 %**
Iron . . . . **13 %**	Folic Acid. . . . . **23 %**	Selenium . . . . . **12 %**
Vitamin E. . . . . . **6 %**	Vitamin B12. . . . **1 %**	Copper. . . . . . . **15 %**
Vitamin K . . . . **10 %**	Pantothenic Acid. **7 %**	Manganese . . . . **21 %**
Vitamin B1. . . . **23 %**		

OTHER BENEFICIAL NUTRIENTS (PER SERVING)

Omega-3 (ALA)	**221 mg**
Choline.	**25 mg**
Beta-Carotene.	**530 mcg**
Lutein & Zeaxanthin.	**123 mcg**
Lycopene.	**1,550 mcg**

GARBANZO AND CAULIFLOWER CRUST PIZZA

6 OR 7 MINI OR 1 LARGE PIZZA • PREPARATION: 30 MINUTES • COOKING: 25 MINUTES • MEDIUM

Although it is not American by origin, few foods have become more commonplace in the U.S. than pizza. Since I wanted to make a truly healthy pizza without wheat or gluten, it took a while for me to figure this out. In the end, I replaced the crust with, of all things, a cruciferous vegetable—cauliflower. It is thin, light, delicious and so healthy. We chose a traditional fresh tomato and basil topping for this recipe, but we also love using a topping of mushrooms, spinach and goat cheese. Feel free to be creative!

Dough:
Cooking oil spray
1½ cups cauliflower
    (approx. ½ head), grated
1½ cups garbanzo flour
1 egg
½ cup mozzarella cheese, shredded
1 clove garlic

1 tbsp. flaxseed
1 oz. fresh or dried oregano
Salt and freshly ground black
    pepper to taste

Topping:
1 cup Tomato Marinara Sauce
(Recipe 33)

Cherry tomatoes, halved
15 fresh mini mozzarella balls
½ cup Parmesan cheese,
    shredded
1 oz. red chili flakes
1 oz. fresh basil, thinly sliced
    à la chiffonade

1 Preheat the oven to 425°. Line a large baking sheet with parchment paper and spray with cooking oil. Chop cauliflower in a food processor until it looks like rice.

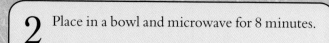

2 Place in a bowl and microwave for 8 minutes.

3 Add the cauliflower to the bowl and mix with the garbanzo flour, egg, shredded mozzarella, garlic, flazseed, oregano, salt and pepper.

4 Mix the mixture with your hands until the dough forms into a ball.

5 Moisten your hands with oil. Spread the dough out with your hands into a single, large pizza crust or multiple mini crusts. The dough will feel quite loose. Lightly spray the top of each crust with cooking oil and bake for 10 minutes. Spread a light layer of marinara sauce on each precooked crust, and add the tomatoes, mozzarella balls, Parmesan cheese, and chili flakes. Cook for 10 minutes until cheese fully melts. Serve hot, garnished with basil à la chiffonade.

Nutrition Information

Serving Size **1 Mini Pizza**   Servings **6**

Calories **237**	Potassium . . . . . . **559 mg**
Calories from fat **79**	Total Carbohydrates . . . **27 g**
Total Fat . . . . **9 g**	Dietary Fiber . . . . **5 g**
Cholesterol . . . . . **44 mg**	Sugars . . . . **5 g**
Sodium . . . . **398 mg**	Protein . . . . **12 g**

Vitamin A . . . . **14 %**	Vitamin B6 . . . . **16 %**
Vitamin A . . . . **62 %**	Folic Acid . . . . **17 %**
Calcium . . . . **22 %**	Vitamin B12 . . . . **6 %**
Iron . . . . **16 %**	Pantothenic Acid . . . . **8 %**
Vitamin D . . . . **2 %**	Phosphorus . . . . **28 %**
Vitamin E . . . . **10 %**	Magnesium . . . . **19 %**
Vitamin K . . . . **14 %**	Zinc . . . . **13 %**
Vitamin B1 . . . . **18 %**	Selenium . . . . **23 %**
Vitamin B2 . . . . **13 %**	Copper . . . . **12 %**
Niacin . . . . **14 %**	Manganese . . . . **70 %**

OTHER BENEFICIAL NUTRIENTS (PER SERVING)

Omega-3 (ALA+EPA+DPA+DHA) . . **57 mg**
Choline . . . . **75 mg**
Beta-Carotene . . . . **310 mcg**
Alpha-Carotene . . . . **21 mcg**
Lutein & Zeaxanthin . . . . **257 mcg**
Lycopene . . . . **6,001 mcg**

PARSNIPS MASHED WITH CARROTS

6 CUPS • PREPARATION: 10 MINUTES • COOKING: 20 MINUTES • EASY

Andrew is careful about eating potatoes, so we often try to find alternatives. The parsnip looks like a large, beige-brown carrot and is rich in many nutrients, as well as fiber. The parsnips and carrots in this recipe provide a healthy alternative to mashed potatoes, and go perfectly alongside our Coq au Vin (Recipe 29). In our Healthy Veggies Cookbook, our Mashed Cauliflower has become a major favorite and I think you will feel the same here. Also, when pureeing the parsnips and carrots, I usually start with 1½ cups of broth and add more until it reaches the desired consistency.

6 parsnips (approx. 1½ lbs.), washed, peeled and cubed

6 carrots (approx. 1 lb.), washed peeled and cubed

2 cups vegetable or chicken broth

1 tbsp. butter

1 tbsp. heavy cream

1 tbsp. almond meal

1 oz. fresh parsley

Salt and freshly ground black pepper to taste

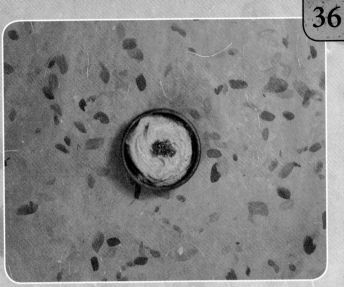

1 Steam the peeled and cubed vegetables for 15 to 20 minutes until soft. Puree in a blender with the broth, butter, cream, and almond meal for approximately 3 minutes.

2 Salt and pepper to taste, and garnish with parsley.

Nutrition Information

Serving Size **1 Cup**   Servings **6**

Calories	94	Potassium	316 mg
Calories from fat	29	Total Carbohydrates	15 g
Total Fat	3 g	Dietary Fiber	4 g
Cholesterol	9 mg	Sugars	5 g
Sodium	366 mg	Protein	1 g

Vitamin A	149 %	Vitamin B6	5 %
Vitamin C	18 %	Folic Acid	10 %
Calcium	3 %	Pantothenic Acid	4 %
Iron	2 %	Phosphorus	6 %
Vitamin D	1 %	Magnesium	5 %
Vitamin E	5 %	Zinc	3 %
Vitamin K	12 %	Selenium	2 %
Vitamin B1	5 %	Copper	4 %
Vitamin B2	3 %	Manganese	16 %
Niacin	4 %		

OTHER BENEFICIAL NUTRIENTS (PER SERVING)

Choline	5 mg
Beta-Carotene	3,543 mcg
Alpha-Carotene	1,485 mcg
Lutein & Zeaxanthin	1,382 mcg

GREEN BEANS WITH WALNUTS AND QUESO FRESCO

8 SERVINGS • PREPARATION: 15 MINUTES • COOKING: 6-8 MINUTES • EASY

Most people do not know that "haricots verts" is French for green beans, so I have been eating and enjoying haricots verts since I was very little. This recipe adds a few new wrinkles with the addition of nonfat yogurt, walnuts and queso fresco (a Spanish and Latin American white cheese). I like the taste of vinegar, but many of you may choose to use less than the ¼ cup recommended below. Steaming for six minutes will make beans that are bright green and a little more firm — the way we like them, but in most French kitchens, they wouldn't dream of serving them firm, since they like their beans soft and a bit overcooked in my opinion.

2 lbs. green beans, ends removed

3 oz. Queso Fresco

½ cup roasted walnuts, chopped

1 garlic clove, crushed

1 shallot, minced

¼ cup or less, red wine vinegar

¼ cup olive oil

¼ cup fat-free yogurt

1 oz. fresh thyme

Salt and freshly ground black pepper to taste

1 Steam the green beans in a steamer basket over boiling water for 6 to 8 minutes, depending on the degree of tenderness desired.

2 Strain the cooked beans and plunge into ice water to retain color.

3 Whisk together the garlic, shallots, vinegar, olive oil, yogurt, thyme, salt and pepper.

4 Toss the dressing with the beans until well mixed.

5 Top with Queso Fresco and walnuts, and serve

Nutrition Information

Servings **8**

Calories	**156**	Potassium	**172 mg**
Calories from fat	**119**	Total Carbohydrates	**6 g**
Total Fat	**13 g**	Dietary Fiber	**2 g**
Cholesterol	**5 mg**	Sugars	**2 g**
Sodium	**50 mg**	Protein	**4 g**

Vitamin A	**9 %**	Vitamin B6	**6 %**
Vitamin C	**12 %**	Folic Acid	**6 %**
Calcium	**7 %**	Vitamin B12	**2 %**
Iron	**5 %**	Pantothenic Acid	**2 %**
Vitamin D	**2 %**	Phosphorus	**8 %**
Vitamin E	**7 %**	Magnesium	**7 %**
Vitamin K	**9 %**	Zinc	**4 %**
Vitamin B1	**5 %**	Selenium	**3 %**
Vitamin B2	**5 %**	Copper	**8 %**
Niacin	**2 %**	Manganese	**20 %**

OTHER BENEFICIAL NUTRIENTS (PER SERVING)

Choline	**13 mg**
Beta-Carotene	**210 mcg**
Alpha-Carotene	**35 mcg**
Lutein & Zeaxanthin	**321 mcg**

QUINOA MAC AND CHEESE WITH CAULIFLOWER BÉCHAMEL

8 CUPS • PREPARATION: 20 MINUTES • COOKING: 25 MINUTES • MEDIUM

Andrew reminded me that most Americans grew up eating Mac and Cheese and like many students, he continued to do so throughout his years of study, because it was so affordable and filling. Since Andrew and I follow a wheat-free diet, we had to find a tasty alternative pasta that was wheat-free. Quinoa or rice pasta worked well and I used mashed cauliflower to add thickness with reduced calories. The peas, mint and a pinch of cayenne add a great array of interesting flavors to what is typically a rich, but less-than-flavorful dish.

1-8 oz. package gluten–free, quinoa macaroni pasta

1 cup fresh (or frozen) peas

½ head cauliflower

1½ cups warm skim milk

3 tbsp. + 1 tsp. butter

¼ cup oat or garbanzo flour (any flour will work)

1 cup Swiss cheese, shredded

½ cup sharp white Cheddar cheese, shredded or cubed

½ cup Gouda cheese, shredded or cubed

A pinch of nutmeg

Salt and freshly ground white pepper to taste

A few mint leaves

A pinch of Cayenne, optional

1 Preheat the oven to 400° and butter your baking dish.

2 Cook the pasta according to the package, which is typically 7 minutes in boiling water with a drop of oil and a pinch of salt. CAUTION: Do not overcook gluten-free pasta as it becomes very mushy. Add the peas for the last 3 minutes of cooking time. Drain in a colander and set aside.

3 Steam the cauliflower in a steamer basket over boiling water for approximately 15 minutes.

4 Mix the cauliflower in a blender with half of the warm milk until very smooth. This should make about 1 to 1½ cups.

5 In a medium saucepan, melt 3 tbsp. of butter and add flour to form a roux. Gradually add the remaining warm milk, constantly whisking for approximately 5 minutes until the sauce thickens.

6 Slowly add all the cheeses, reserving a little of each cheese for the topping (½ cup combined).

7 Once the cheese thoroughly melts, add the smooth cauliflower mixture, and the nutmeg, salt and pepper. Cook for approximately 3 additional minutes.

8 Place the macaroni and peas in the buttered baking dish and pour the sauce over the pasta.

9 Top with the reserved cheese and bake for 25 minutes.

10 Garnish with fresh mint and cayenne, and serve.

Nutrition Information

Serving Size **1/2 Cup**   Servings **16**

Calories	**223**	Potassium	**261 mg**
Calories from fat	**116**	Total Carbohydrates	**15 g**
Total Fat	**13 g**	Dietary Fiber	**5 g**
Cholesterol	**38 mg**	Sugars	**3 g**
Sodium	**286 mg**	Protein	**11 g**

Vitamin A	**10 %**	Vitamin B6	**11 %**
Vitamin C	**27 %**	Folic Acid	**14 %**
Calcium	**22 %**	Vitamin B12	**11 %**
Iron	**7 %**	Pantothenic Acid	**6 %**
Vitamin D	**3 %**	Phosphorus	**27 %**
Vitamin E	**3 %**	Magnesium	**14 %**
Vitamin K	**9 %**	Zinc	**11 %**
Vitamin B1	**10 %**	Selenium	**10 %**
Vitamin B2	**21 %**	Copper	**10 %**
Niacin	**4 %**	Manganese	**221 %**

OTHER BENEFICIAL NUTRIENTS (PER SERVING)

Omega-3 (ALA+EPA+DPA+DHA)	**8 mg**
Choline	**38 mg**
Beta-Carotene	**63 mcg**
Alpha-Carotene	**2 mcg**
Lutein & Zeaxanthin	**251 mcg**

ZUCCHINI PARMESAN FRIES

8 SERVINGS • PREPARATION: 10 MINUTES • COOKING: 20 MINUTES • EASY

This is a simple and much healthier version of French fries. With this recipe, we have eliminated both the potatoes and the frying and of course, so many of the calories! We serve them as both an hors d'oeuvres or as a side dish with our delicious homemade Tomato Marinara Sauce (Recipe 33). Andrew often dips them in Dijon mustard, either on its own or mixed with a little bit of light mayonnaise and honey.

Olive oil cooking spray

4 zucchini

1 tsp. garlic powder

⅓ cup Parmesan cheese,
    finely shredded

Salt and freshly ground black
    pepper to taste

1 tsp. paprika

Red chili pepper flakes,
    optional

1 Preheat the oven to 450°. Line a baking sheet with parchment paper or tin foil and spray with olive oil. Trim off the end of each zucchini, cut in half crosswise, and then cut each half lengthwise into 4 strips for a total of 32 pieces.

2 Place the zucchini on the lined baking sheet and spray with olive oil. Sprinkle with salt and pepper, garlic powder, Parmesan cheese and paprika. Bake for approximately 20 minutes until nicely golden.

3 Serve immediately, hot out of the oven! I like to top them with a few chili pepper flakes. You may also serve with a side of marinara sauce.

Nutrition Information

Serving Size **4 Fries**　　　　　　　　　　　Servings **8**

Calories	**37**	Potassium	**275 mg**
Calories from fat	**12**	Total Carbohydrates	**4 g**
Total Fat	**1 g**	Dietary Fiber	**1 g**
Cholesterol	**2 mg**	Sugars	**3 g**
Sodium	**65 mg**	Protein	**3 g**

Vitamin A	**9 %**	Folic Acid	**6 %**
Vitamin C	**30 %**	Vitamin B12	**1 %**
Calcium	**6 %**	Pantothenic Acid	**2 %**
Iron	**3 %**	Phosphorus	**6 %**
Vitamin E	**1 %**	Magnesium	**5 %**
Vitamin K	**5 %**	Zinc	**3 %**
Vitamin B1	**3 %**	Selenium	**2 %**
Vitamin B2	**6 %**	Copper	**3 %**
Niacin	**3 %**	Manganese	**9 %**
Vitamin B6	**9 %**		

OTHER BENEFICIAL NUTRIENTS (PER SERVING)

Choline	**10 mg**
Beta-Carotene	**244 mcg**
Alpha-Carotene	**2 mcg**
Lutein & Zeaxanthin	**2,167 mcg**

CARROT, RAISIN AND OAT BREAD

15 SLICES • PREPARATION: 25 MINUTES • COOKING: 55-60 MINUTES • MEDIUM

To truly be a "sandwich," our Almond Butter and Jam or AB&J (Recipe 11) needed some bread, so I thought I would create an easy recipe that is both wheat and gluten free. This is simple to make at home and you can feel free to be creative with the ingredients. For instance, you can replace the carrots with grated zucchinis, chopped dates, chopped figs, blueberries, or any fruit or vegetable of your choice. It is delicious! Andrew often has a slice with breakfast or as a snack throughout the day — sometimes with our almond butter and jam.

Cooking oil spray

1½ cups oat flour, leveled with a
    knife

½ cup oat bran

1 tsp. baking powder

1 tsp. baking soda

¾ cup brown sugar or agave

1 tsp. cinnamon

½ tsp. salt

1 egg

¾ cup low-fat milk
    (I prefer buttermilk
    or almond milk)

1 cup carrots, grated

½ cup pecans, crushed

½ cup raisins, crushed

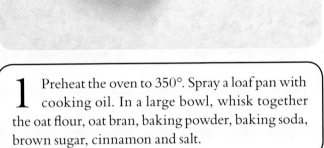

1 Preheat the oven to 350°. Spray a loaf pan with cooking oil. In a large bowl, whisk together the oat flour, oat bran, baking powder, baking soda, brown sugar, cinnamon and salt.

2 Whisk the egg and milk together in a small bowl.

3 Grate the carrots and crush the pecans and raisins.

4 With a rubber spatula, combine the wet and dry ingredients. Lightly fold in the carrots, raisins and pecans. DO NOT OVERMIX!

5 Pour the batter into the loaf pan smoothing the top with a spatula or knife. Bake for 55 to 60 minutes until golden. Test for doneness by inserting a toothpick, which will come out clean when the bread is done.

6 Place on a rack to cool before slicing and serving.

Nutrition Information

Serving Size **1 Slice**   Servings **15**

Calories	187	Potassium	243 mg
Calories from fat	37	Total Carbohydrates	34 g
Total Fat	4 g	Dietary Fiber	2 g
Cholesterol	11 mg	Sugars	22 g
Sodium	180 mg	Protein	4 g

Vitamin A	25 %	Folic Acid	3 %
Vitamin C	1 %	Vitamin B12	1 %
Calcium	4 %	Pantothenic Acid	2 %
Iron	6 %	Phosphorus	14 %
Vitamin D	1 %	Magnesium	9 %
Vitamin E	1 %	Zinc	5 %
Vitamin B1	10 %	Selenium	9 %
Vitamin B2	5 %	Copper	8 %
Niacin	2 %	Manganese	42 %
Vitamin B6	4 %		

OTHER BENEFICIAL NUTRIENTS (PER SERVING)

Omega-3 (ALA+EPA+DPA+DHA)	7 mg
Choline	18 mg
Beta-Carotene	609 mcg
Alpha-Carotene	255 mcg
Lutein & Zeaxanthin	59 mcg

SIMPLE AND EASY CORNBREAD

15 SERVINGS • PREPARATION: 20 MINUTES • COOKING: 25 MINUTES • MEDIUM

If you are making this cornbread for stuffing, the most difficult part of the recipe will be to keep everyone from eating it beforehand! It is only safe if I know Andrew is not around. I almost always make my own cornbread, but if you would rather use a "package mix," Bob's Red Mill® makes a great, gluten-free version and Pamela's® Cornbread & Muffin Mix works very well too. You will notice that ours contains little to no added sugar or fat.

1¾ cups cornmeal (stoneground)

1 tbsp. baking powder

1 tsp. baking soda

1 tsp. salt

2 eggs, beaten

4 tbsp. melted butter

1 cup fat-free buttermilk

⅔ cup skim milk

1 tbsp. honey

1 Preheat oven to 450°. In a medium bowl, combine the cornmeal, baking powder, baking soda and salt.

2 In a small bowl, combine the eggs, melted butter, buttermilk, skim milk and honey.

3 Quickly whisk the wet ingredients into the dry being careful not to over mix.

4 Pour the batter into a buttered dish and bake for 20 to 25 minutes until lightly brown on the top and a knife (or toothpick) comes out dry. Carefully cut and serve.

Nutrition Information

Serving Size **1 Slice**   Servings **15**

Calories	113	Potassium	300 mg
Calories from fat	42	Total Carbohydrates	14 g
Total Fat	5 g	Dietary Fiber	1 g
Cholesterol	46 mg	Sugars	3 g
Sodium	309 mg	Protein	3 g

Vitamin A	4 %	Vitamin B12	3 %
Calcium	4 %	Pantothenic Acid	3 %
Iron	4 %	Phosphorus	22 %
Vitamin D	3 %	Magnesium	6 %
Vitamin E	1 %	Zinc	3 %
Vitamin B1	5 %	Selenium	9 %
Vitamin B2	7 %	Copper	2 %
Niacin	3 %	Manganese	4 %
Vitamin B6	3 %		
Folic Acid	2 %		

OTHER BENEFICIAL NUTRIENTS (PER SERVING)

Omega-3 (ALA+EPA+DPA+DHA)	25 mg
Choline	38 mg
Beta-Carotene	20 mcg
Alpha-Carotene	9 mcg
Lutein & Zeaxanthin	243 mcg

APPLE CRUMBLE COCOTTE

6 SERVINGS • PREPARATION: 15 MINUTES • COOKING: 25 MINUTES • MEDIUM

This is my healthier version of apple pie. It is quite versatile and you can feel free to substitute walnuts for the pecans or any flour to replace the almond meal. I like making it in small individual servings, since it is really the only way to control portions and caloric intake. Because the French usually glaze their apple pies with apricot jam, I added apricot preserves (no sugar added) to the apples for a little extra sweetness. If it is not sweet enough for your taste, you can add a small amount of agave or sugar to the apple mixture. Be very careful not to blend your whipped cream too long as the mixture can quickly turn into butter.

Apple mixture:

3 Jonathan apples,
   peeled and cubed

1 tsp. cinnamon

Juice of a lemon

1 tsp. vanilla extract

½ cup sugar-free apricot preserves

Crumble:

½ cup quick-cooking rolled oats

½ cup almond meal

1 tsp. cinnamon

2 tbsp. agave syrup

½ cup pecans, crushed

2 tbsp. butter, melted

1 tsp. vanilla extract

Fresh whipped cream:

1 cup heavy whipping cream

1½ tbsp. powdered sugar

1 tsp. vanilla extract

Zest of a lime

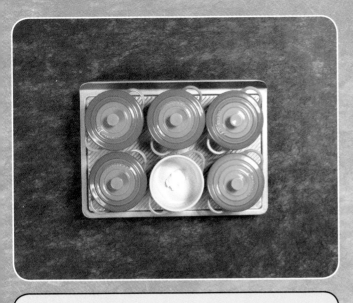

1 Preheat the oven to 350°. Butter six small cocottes (covered Dutch oven) or a 6" x 9" baking dish.

2 In a large bowl, mix the cubed apples with the cinnamon, lemon juice, vanilla and preserves.

3 Prepare the crumble by combining the oats, almond meal, cinnamon, agave, crushed pecans, melted butter and vanilla extract. Mix well.

4 Transfer the apple mixture into your cocottes or baking dish.

5 Top the apple with the crumble and bake for 25 minutes. Cool before serving.

6 Beat cold whipping cream, sugar and vanilla with an electric mixer for approximately 5 minutes until soft peaks form at the top. Top the cooled apples and crumble with the whipped cream, and serve. Garnish with lime zest.

Nutrition Information

Serving Size **1 Cocotte**   Servings **6**

Calories	251	Potassium	205 mg
Calories from fat	107	Total Carbohydrates	33 g
Total Fat	12 g	Dietary Fiber	5 g
Cholesterol	10 mg	Sugars	15 g
Sodium	39 mg	Protein	3 g

Vitamin A	4 %	Vitamin B6	6 %
Vitamin C	14 %	Folic Acid	3 %
Calcium	3 %	Pantothenic Acid	3 %
Iron	6 %	Phosphorus	9 %
Vitamin D	1 %	Magnesium	10 %
Vitamin E	3 %	Zinc	6 %
Vitamin K	3 %	Selenium	6 %
Vitamin B1	10 %	Copper	9 %
Vitamin B2	6 %	Manganese	45 %
Niacin	4 %		

OTHER BENEFICIAL NUTRIENTS (PER SERVING)

Choline	14 mg
Beta-Carotene	52 mcg
Alpha-Carotene	6 mcg
Lutein & Zeaxanthin	181 mcg

STRAWBERRY PARFAITS

6 SERVINGS • PREPARATION: 15 MINUTES • EASY

This is a wonderful, fresh and easy dessert! It's very low in calories and satisfies our craving for sweets every time. It works well even if you are dieting. You can replace the strawberries with blueberries or any mixed berries; I use whatever I have in the refrigerator. You can also make the yogurt by mixing plain fat-free yogurt with our Strawberry Jam (Recipe 11) or any of your favorite flavors. Personally, I like creamy Greek strawberry yogurt. We resist the temptation, but if you want it sweeter, you can always add a hint of agave or honey.

3 cups unsweetened
strawberry yogurt
(½ cup per glass)

3 cups strawberries, chopped
(½ cup per glass)

1 tbsp. flaxseeds (optional)

⅔ cup roasted almonds, sliced

Zest of 1 lime

1 oz. fresh mint leaves

Whipped cream (optional)

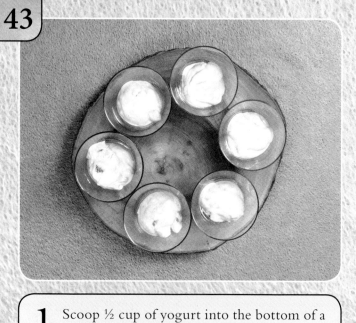

1   Scoop ½ cup of yogurt into the bottom of a small glass.

2   Place ½ cup of strawberries on top of the yogurt.

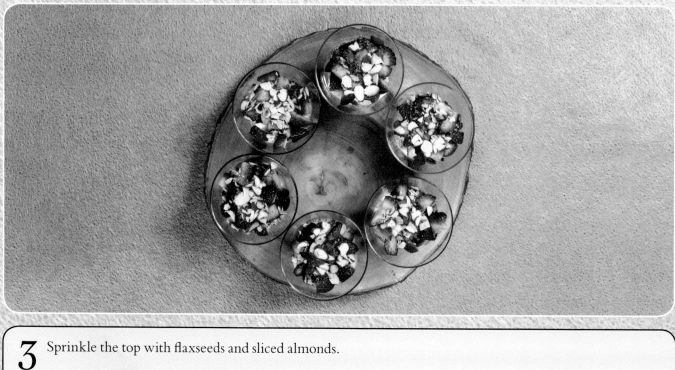

3   Sprinkle the top with flaxseeds and sliced almonds.

4 Top with whipped cream (optional), and garnish with lime zest and mint leaves.

Nutrition Information

Serving Size 1 Parfait   **Servings 6**

Calories	178	Potassium	418 mg
Calories from fat	90	Total Carbohydrates	15 g
Total Fat	10 g	Dietary Fiber	4 g
Cholesterol	16 mg	Sugars	10 g
Sodium	59 mg	Protein	7 g

Vitamin A	7 %	Folic Acid	10 %
Vitamin C	77 %	Vitamin B12	8 %
Calcium	20 %	Pantothenic Acid	7 %
Iron	8 %	Phosphorus	20 %
Vitamin D	1 %	Magnesium	16 %
Vitamin E	15 %	Zinc	9 %
Vitamin B1	7 %	Selenium	5 %
Vitamin B2	18 %	Copper	9 %
Niacin	4 %	Manganese	32 %
Vitamin B6	5 %		

OTHER BENEFICIAL NUTRIENTS (PER SERVING)

Choline	30 mg
Beta-Carotene	12 mcg
Lutein & Zeaxanthin	31 mcg

MINI CHEESECAKE WITH DATE AND OAT CRUST

24 SERVINGS • PREPARATION: 20 MINUTES • COOKING: 20 MINUTES • MEDIUM

We should enjoy what we eat, but when it comes to dessert, Andrew always reminds me that it's all about portion control and smart ingredient choices. These small servings provide the perfect delicious portion to enjoy and because of the choice of ingredients, the level of sugars, carbohydrates and fats make this a healthy treat. We serve them with a dollop of our Strawberry Jam (Recipe 11), but any jam or fresh fruit (especially berries) works fine.

Crust:
Coconut oil cooking spray
¼ cup almond meal
2 dates, pitted
¼ cup oat flour
¼ cup walnuts, chopped
2 tbsp. melted butter

2 tbsp. palm coconut sugar
  (or brown sugar)
1 tsp. cinnamon

Filling:
8 oz. ⅓-fat-free cream cheese
2 tbsp. light sour cream

2 tbsp. cornstarch
1 tsp. vanilla extract
2 tbsp. white sugar
Zest of a lemon
2 eggs
½ cup strawberry jam

1 Preheat the oven to 350°. Place paper liners into mini-muffin baking tins and spray with coconut cooking oil. In a high-speed blender, mix all of the crust ingredients and pulse until smooth.

2 In a large bowl, mix the cream cheese, sour cream, cornstarch, vanilla extract, white sugar and lemon zest. Once the mixture is smooth, add the eggs one at a time.

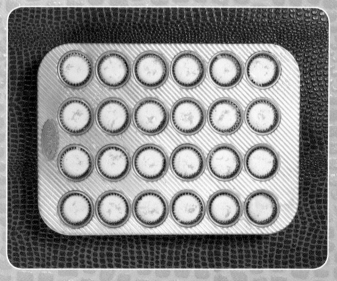

3 Place approximately 1 teaspoon of the crust into the bottom of the lined muffin tins and spread thinly with your fingers.

4 Add a tablespoon of the filling on top of each crust and top with lemon zest.

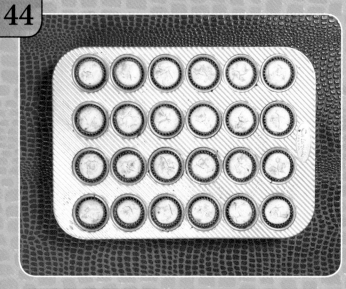

5 Bake for approximately 20 minutes until lightly golden.

6 Garnish each mini cheesecake with a dollop of strawberry jam and serve. Refrigerate leftover muffins, if there are any!

Nutrition Information

Serving Size **1 Mini Cheesecake**   Servings **24**

Calories	49	Potassium	28 mg
Calories from fat	15	Total Carbohydrates	8 g
Total Fat	2 g	Dietary Fiber	0 g
Cholesterol	16 mg	Sugars	4 g
Sodium	9 mg	Protein	1 g

Vitamin A	1 %	Vitamin B12	1 %
Vitamin C	1 %	Pantothenic Acid	1 %
Calcium	1 %	Phosphorus	2 %
Iron	1 %	Magnesium	2 %
Vitamin D	1 %	Zinc	1 %
Vitamin B1	1 %	Selenium	3 %
Vitamin B2	2 %	Copper	2 %
Niacin	1 %	Manganese	6 %
Vitamin B6	1 %		
Folic Acid	1 %		

OTHER BENEFICIAL NUTRIENTS (PER SERVING)

Choline	14 mg
Beta–Carotene	2 mcg
Alpha–Carotene	1 mcg
Lutein & Zeaxanthin	41 mcg

INDEX